More American Furniture Treasures
1620-1840

"One Nation Indivisible—"

Medallion of
GEORGE WASHINGTON

A. Demarest, Sculptor

·*More*·
AMERICAN
FURNITURE
TREASURES

1620-1840

An Anthology with Photographs
Measured Drawings
and Eclectic Discussions.

BY LESTER MARGON, A.I.D.

ARCHITECTURAL BOOK PUBLISHING CO.

New York

Published simultaneously in Canada by
Saunders, of Toronto, Ltd., Don Mills, Ontario

ISBN: 8038-0163-7

Library of Congress Catalog Card Number: 70-150013

Printed in the United States of America

CONTENTS

FOREWORD

THIS book is not intended to serve as a history of furniture. However, it will prove a valuable and useful work for interior designers, home craftsmen, architects, collectors, furniture manufacturers and any others interested in American furniture. We need no longer be content with the conventional austerity of furniture manuals, for the story of American furniture is thrilling and exciting, and the author has endeavored to portray it as such. Names, periods, and dates have been included, as they are important to many people. But most important is the spirit that has created this splendid composite of rewarding furniture that is our heritage.

In this book is included a diversity of material ranging from the purely historical to the metaphysical. By shooting arrows into the air, it is hoped that some may penetrate the sensibility of many who may have forgotten the legacy that is ours to enjoy. Seven eclectic and often controversial chapters express the personal contentions of the author on subjects relating to the main theme. It is hoped that this text will enliven interest in American furniture treasures as a motivating force in interior design for today. The purpose of this book is for study, contemplation and inspiration. All of the pieces included are choice examples of Early American furniture that are preserved in museum collections and are included here by special permission. A learned authority has commented that the good selection in Mr. Margon's books and his drawings exceed anything heretofore attempted in this country; another called one of Mr. Margon's previous books "an excellent compendium of source material."

Curators throughout the country are constantly receiving requests for permission to copy pieces in their furniture collections. They are reluctant to give this permission indiscriminately. Therefore, the paucity of such measured material would suggest that this book would be a welcome addition to any school or public library, and for the personal use of anyone directly involved in the field. It offers a wide range of American material. A homeowner, for example, interested in purchasing an oval dining room table with dropped leaves, would do well to first acquaint himself with period examples.

Although this volume is useful as a reference work and for rewarding reading in the field of social history, it will of course also be of practical value for persons concerned with American antique furniture. Good traditional design is always acceptable. The book is full of authentic material but not the same pieces too often repeated in so many furniture manuals. There are fifty measured drawings executed with meticulous care, with accompanying photographs and descriptive commentary. Here are shown front and side elevations, plans, construction, and enlarged details when deemed necessary. Included are one hundred selected photographs of related pieces of furniture, many of which were taken specially for this volume.

Today the manufacture of reproductions of antique furniture plays an important role in the furniture industry of this country. This is proof of the worthiness of the products of the colonial craftsmen. The most salient recommendation is the simplicity of many of the examples. These craftsmen were determined to create new images that fitted into the unfettered life of the new country. In many instances their work surpassed the European prototypes in beauty.

A great deal of American antique furniture is being faked so expertly that in many cases it comes close to fooling the connoisseurs. This is regrettable, for there are dealers who cannot tell the difference. In any case, many, in ignorance or by intention, offer such pieces as genuine antiques at fabulous prices. Therefore we suggest that purchasers of antiques patronize only reputable dealers who vouch for the authenticity of the objects and can supply a signed statement.

For the general public there are many fine reproductions being made by reputable manufacturers. They can be purchased at reasonable prices. They are honestly presented and worthy of your consideration. Some, such as Kittinger, are offering furniture adaptations from the Williamsburg Restoration. In purchasing furniture for the home, give the matter due consideration. Furniture is often a lifetime possession and should be a daily contributor to your well-being and happiness.

MUSEUMS REPRESENTED IN THIS VOLUME

The Art Institute of Chicago, Chicago, Illinois
The Brooklyn Museum, Brooklyn, New York
Colonial Williamsburg, Williamsburg, Virginia
The Cooper-Hewitt Museum of Decorative Arts and Design,
    The Smithsonian Institution, New York
The Detroit Institute of Arts, Detroit, Michigan
The Essex Institute, Salem, Massachusetts
The Fine Arts Society Museum, San Diego, California
The Henry E. Huntington Art Gallery and Library,
    San Marino, California
The Henry Francis du Pont Winterthur Museum,
    Winterthur, Delaware
The Heritage Foundation, Deerfield, Massachusetts
The Los Angeles County Museum of Art, Los Angeles, California
The Metropolitan Museum of Art, New York, New York
The Museum of Art, Rhode Island School of Design,
    Providence, Rhode Island
The M. H. de Young Memorial Museum, San Francisco, California
The Museum of the City of New York, New York, New York
The Museum of Fine Arts, Boston, Massachusetts
Old Sturbridge Village, Sturbridge, Massachusetts
The Philadelphia Museum of Art, Philadelphia, Pennsylvania
The Shaker Museum, Old Chatham, New York
The Shelburne Museum, Shelburne, Vermont
The Wadsworth Atheneum, Hartford, Connecticut

The Louvre, Paris, France
The Victoria and Albert Museum, London, England

ACKNOWLEDGMENTS

I AM especially grateful to the museums throughout the country who have enthusiastically cooperated in the preparation of this volume. Their willingness to permit the sketching of choice pieces in their furniture collections and to supply photographs for reproduction bespeaks a healthy comradeship between the museum, students and workers seeking greater knowledge and understanding of American furniture treasures. A few photographs from a British and a French museum have been included for comparison.

All these courtesies offered by museums, art commissions, park services and by several magazines, are sincerely appreciated.

Lester Margon, A.I.D.

WE are also grateful to the following organizations and publications:

The Art Commission of the City of New York
The National Park Service — New York
Workbench Magazine
Antiques Magazine
Interior Design Magazine
Interiors Magazine

LIST OF ILLUSTRATIONS

(Asterisks indicate photographs accompanied by measured drawings.)

INTRODUCTION

As an introduction to American furniture, we present first a selection of ten measured drawings, with accompanying photographs of each piece of furniture. Grouped with them are photographs of related pieces and interiors, with descriptive and informative text. This section will show the high calibre of American furniture that may be found in the museum collections throughout this country. The variety is tremendous, the quality superb. These are some of the finest pieces of antique furniture. The acquisition of fine antiques entails a definite obligation to use them for the viewing and appreciation of the public. These American furniture treasures are our heritage. They are a national benefaction which we can all enjoy.

HEPPLEWHITE SECRETARY

ESSEX INSTUTE · SALEM

Circa · 1809 ·

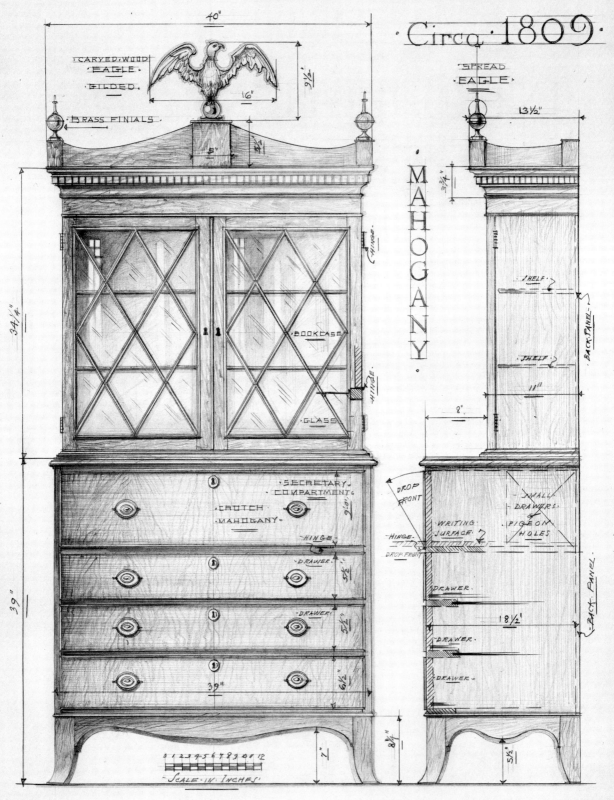

· CARVED · WOOD · EAGLE · GILDED ·

· BRASS FINIALS ·

16"

9½"

40"

· SPREAD · EAGLE ·

13½"

3¾"

· MAHOGANY ·

· HINGE ·

· BOOKCASE ·

· SHELF ·

· SHELF ·

11"

· BACK · PANEL ·

· HINGE ·

· GLASS ·

8"

34¼"

· SECRETARY · COMPARTMENT ·

· CROTCH · MAHOGANY ·

2"

· HINGE ·

· DRAWER ·

5½"

· DRAWER ·

5½"

· DRAWER ·

6½"

39"

· DROP · FRONT ·

· WRITING · SURFACE ·

· HINGE ·

· DROP FRONT ·

· SMALL · DRAWERS · & · PIGEON · HOLES ·

· DRAWER ·

18½"

· DRAWER ·

· DRAWER ·

· BACK · PANEL ·

39"

8¼"

7"

0 1 2 3 4 5 6 7 8 9 10 11 12

· SCALE · IN · INCHES ·

5½"

· FRONT · VIEW ·

· END · VIEW ·

· Measured & Drawn by Lester Margon ·

HEPPLEWHITE SECRETARY

Essex Institute, Salem

The Essex Institute in Salem, Massachusetts, was formed in 1846. The museum contains one of the largest collections of antique furniture in the United States illustrating the Colonial and Federal life of the people. The John Ward House, on the premises, was built in 1684. It shows the characteristic architectural features and is furnished in the manner of the times. It was our pleasure and privilege to sketch the magnificent Hepplewhite straight-front secretary from Salem, *circa* 1809. In it is a drop-front desk compartment with three drawers below, all of equal size. The doors of the separate bookcase above are divided into lozenge-shaped panes. The well-defined cornice is ornamented by a row of dentils. The shaped cresting above has a spread eagle surmounting the center. The eagle is of the McIntire type, so popular in all the forms of decorative art during the Federal period. These years, at the turn of the 19th century, witnessed a decided change in furniture design. The influence of architectural details was profound as is witnessed in the work of Samuel McIntire in Salem. The question whether or not he was a carver has never been determined. If not, he certainly did supervise a tremendous amount of interior design in the vicinity. This is also true of Thomas Jefferson and Charles Bulfinch. Note the exquisitely turned brass finials at the top and the oval shaped brass pulls that are usually found on pieces of the Hepplewhite tradition.

15

OVAL MIRROR

Metropolitan Museum of Art   Sansbury-Mills Fund, 1952

This oval mirror in the Chippendale style dates from the third quarter of the 18th century. The frame is carved of mahogany with gilt and the spread eagle at the pinnacle is the symbol of the early years of the Republic, when there was hardly an object in the American home that did not use this versatile eagle for decoration. The patriotic citizens of the young nation favored the eagle in various postures, William Barton depict-ing the eagle on the coins as a heraldic bird. Lead-ing cabinetmakers and artisans capitalized on the tremendous commercial value the eagle had at this time. A splendid example, this mirror would add to the beauty of the finest American living room. It measures 45" high x 20½" wide. Surrounded by a profusion of scrolls, cut-outs and drop orna-ments on the sides, with the eagle surmounting it, the mirror is both pretentious and picturesque.

SECRETARY WITH BOMBÉ BASE

Metropolitan Museum of Art, New York   The Kennedy Fund, 1918

This Chippendale mahogany secretary with bombé base shows the use of Rococo forms and details. It is from Massachusetts, *circa* 1760-1775. The combination is a rarity and is typical of the work done exclusively in the Boston and Salem area. This combination piece resembles closely one in the Dwight Barnard House in Old Deerfield, Massachusetts, and is included here for comparison. This piece attests to the skill of the cabinetmaker who achieved such grace and balance in a tremendous piece that otherwise might have proven ponderous. The broken architectural pediment and the graceful lineation of the bookcase doors, held in place by the side pilasters, all break up the tremendous mass. Of course, the bombé base is what gives this secretary distinction. Note that the double curved profile is augmented by the block panels in the front. This is certainly a prodigious performance.

EAGLE·BACK·SIDE·CHAIR·

·MUSEUM·OF·THE·CITY·OF·NEW·YORK·

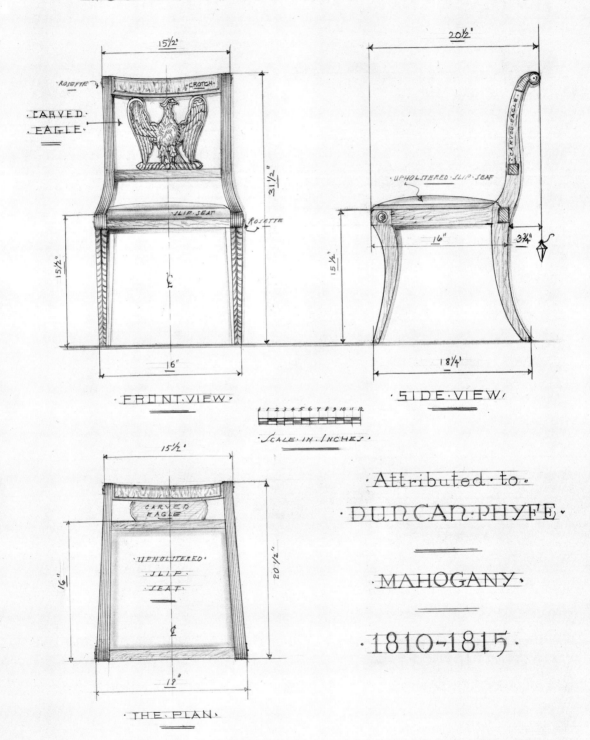

·ROSETTE·

·CROTCH·

·CARVED·
·EAGLE·

·SLIP·SEAT·

·Rosette·

15½"

31½"

15½"

16"

·FRONT·VIEW·

20½"

·UPHOLSTERED·SLIP·SEAT·

·CARVED·EAGLE·

16"

3¾"

15½"

18¼"

·SIDE·VIEW·

0 1 2 3 4 5 6 7 8 9 10 11 12

·SCALE·IN·INCHES·

15½"

·CARVED·
·EAGLE·

·UPHOLSTERED·
·SLIP·
·SEAT·

16"

20½"

18"

·THE·PLAN·

·Attributed·to·

·DUNCAN·PHYFE·

·MAHOGANY·

·1810~1815·

Measured·&·Drawn·by·Lester Margon·

EAGLE BACK SIDE CHAIR

Museum of the City of New York   *Bequest of Mrs. Henry O. Tallmadge*

During the years of the birth of our country, the American Eagle had a conspicous place in the new nation's heraldry, appearing as the central motif on the Great Seal. On coins, and every form of decoration, the eagle spread its wings. Samuel McIntire's mantels and architectural trim have never been surpassed in the exceptional delicacy in which the eagle was portrayed. In this side chair in mahogany, *circa* 1810-1815, attributed to Duncan Phyfe, the carved eagle is the center of interest as the back splat. This chair was made for Mayor De Witt Clinton, later Governor of New York State. Besides being an elegant side chair,

this piece is a symbol of the patriotic fervor that pervaded the land during this period. The bird found its place on embroideries, and all forms of handiwork and personal adornments. Glassblowers pressed the image onto flasks, cups and beakers, and it was painted onto china and pottery. In castings it appeared as the crowning glory of flagpoles, and surmounted, carved and gilded, many mirrors. Duncan Phyfe used the eagle as the central motif of the carvings on the back panels of his famous sofas. The eagle was beloved as "The Bird of Freedom" by early Americans.

EAGLE BACK CHAIR

Art Institute of Chicago   Gift of Mrs. Emily Crane Chadbourne

This early 19th century chair in mahogany is from the School of Duncan Phyfe. The carved eagle splat reflects the influence the Federal form of government exerted on all the arts at this time. Note that the top rail is slightly curved and the back posts finish in a scroll at the top. Duncan Phyfe was the foremost cabinet-maker of the Federal period. His furniture was most graceful, emphasizing delicacy of line and fine detail with exquisite carving. The American flag was the favored motif in furniture and all household accessories, with stars and stripes used wherever possible. Patriotic symbols prevailed in an orgy of patriotism that found expression in all types of decalcomanias and often on the upper panels of Sheraton mirrors.

NEW REPUBLIC SIDE CHAIR

Art Institute of Chicago   Gift of the Antiquarian Society

This mahogany side chair, possibly from New Jersey, *circa* 1790, is a good example of the trend in furniture design and decoration during the years of the New Republic. It was then that the eagle was the favored symbol in all forms of embellishments. The bird found its way to the Great Seal of the United States, the tops of mirrors and clocks, to Staffordshire ware and Lowestoft, brass fenders and what not. Many chairs and tables incorporated carved eagles as the central motif, and there are many examples of chairs where the eagle formed the design of the back as in this very attractive side chair. The eagle was also prominent on cotton prints, wallpapers, overdoor ornaments, butter moulds and certainly on all Federal documents.

TILT·TOP·TABLE · Southern · 1760

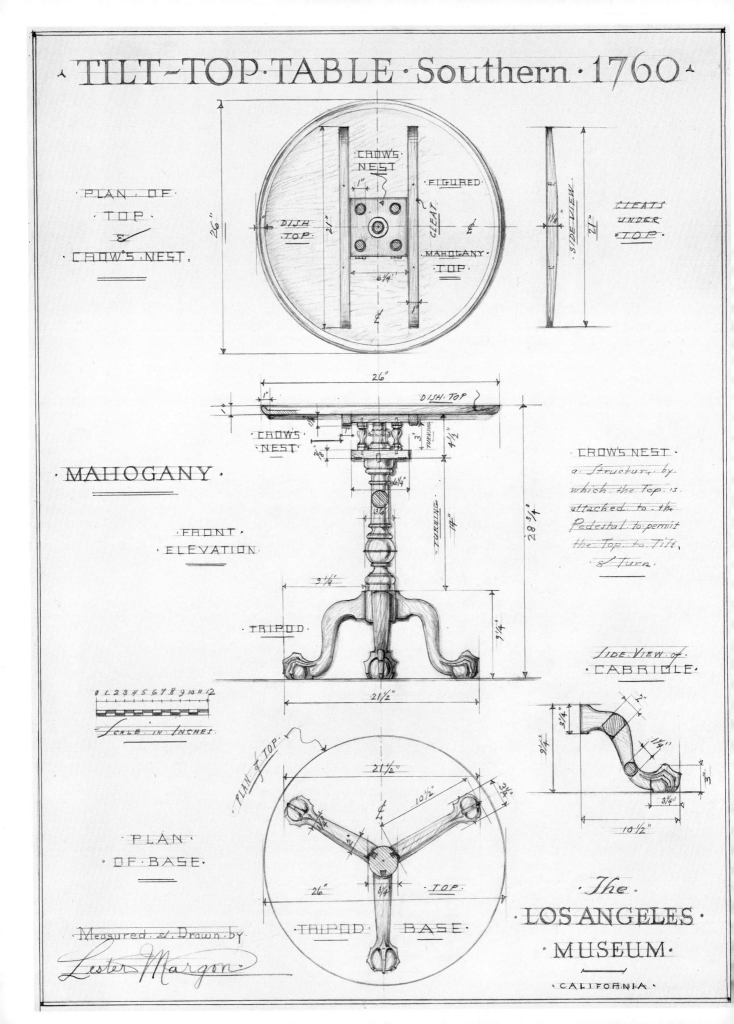

PLAN · OF
· TOP ·
&
· CROW'S · NEST ·

CROW'S
NEST

FIGURED

CLEAT

DISH
TOP

MAHOGANY
· TOP ·

26"

21"

6¼"

SIDE·VIEW·

21"

CLEATS
UNDER
· TOP ·

· MAHOGANY ·

· FRONT ·
ELEVATION

· TRIPOD ·

26"

DISH·TOP

CROW'S
NEST

TURNING

4½"

6¼"

3½"

14"

28¾"

9½"

9¼"

21½"

CROW'S NEST
a Structure by
which the Top is
attached to the
Pedestal to permit
the Top to Tilt
& Turn.

· SIDE·VIEW· of
· CABRIOLE ·

2"

3¼"

9¼"

1¼"

3"

3¼"

10½"

0 1 2 3 4 5 6 7 8 9 10 11 12
· SCALE · IN · INCHES ·

· PLAN ·
· OF · BASE ·

· PLAN · of · TOP ·

21½"

10½"

¾"

26"

· TOP ·

¾"

· TRIPOD · BASE ·

· Measured & Drawn by ·

Lester Margon

· The ·
LOS ANGELES
· MUSEUM ·
· CALIFORNIA ·

TILT-TOP TABLE

Los Angeles County Museum of Art   *Purchase of the Dennis Bequest*

This is a particularly attractive tilt-top table from the collection of the Los Angeles County Museum of Art. Of Southern origin, its date is *circa* 1760. The dish top is held in place by a lower crow's nest consisting of a series of small turnings. It is constructed so that the top can tilt or revolve. The design is certainly Chippendale with the turned pedestal supported by three cabriole legs with ball-and-claw feet. The profile and character of the legs are certainly articulate. Many of these tilt-top tables were used in the drawing rooms for the service of tea. When this was accomplished the top was lowered and the table either removed or set aside. The richness of the mahogany in this instance required no further elaboration. The eloquence of the turned pedestal is self-evident. Unfortunately the museum has recently discontinued its furniture and decorative arts section. This is truly lamentable. There seem to be differences in its direction as to just what type of the museum it should be. We hope that the former decorative arts gallery will be soon reinstated, as the collection of furniture was small but important.

SEWING TABLE

Metropolitan Museum of Art, New York   Gift of Mrs. Russell Sage, 1909

This little mahogany sewing table, *circa* 1785, is in the Sheraton style. In Colonial times, sewing tables were a part of the furnishings of the living room. Today they are in secluded areas of the house. This was not so in Colonial times. The sewing table played a prominent rôle in the living room where the ladies assembled to do their sewing, accompanied by the most recent gossip. It was part of the environment. Small pieces of such furniture are rare. This model has a hinged top which, when lifted reveals a carefully divided interior for the placement of sewing materials. The top drawer is necessarily false but it does complete the front elevation. Below is a single drawer for additional sewing materials. The slender tapered legs produce a sense of suspension which is supplemented by the shaped plan. Only recently have antique sewing tables been sought after. Their real worth is being appreciated as a valuable contribution to American furniture design. Of course, this piece might be used as a vanity table with the inside of the top mirrored or a small mirror hung above. It has been suggested that it might serve as a student's desk. However, the original purpose was a sewing table and it is best suited as such. Again this piece is the gift of Mrs. Russell Sage, 1909, to the American Wing and is much appreciated.

TILT-TOP TABLE

The Philadelphia Museum of Art

This mahogany Chippendale tilt-top table from Philadelphia, Pennsylvania, *circa* 1780, is a masterpiece. The table is well balanced and the three outstretching cabriole legs create a firm base. The carving is superlative, especially on the knees of the cabriole legs that end in ball-and-claw feet. The pedestal post is majestic in contour and carving. The serrated edge of the piecrust top is well delineated. Beneath is an adequate birdcage to permit the top to tilt easily. There are so many tilt-top tables about, but many of them are uninspired and anemic. This model is bold and sturdy. It invites being used with confidence in the design and proportions. In fact, this is one of the finest tilt-top tables that has come to our attention.

DESK Used by GEORGE WASHINGTON
NEW YORK CITY HALL

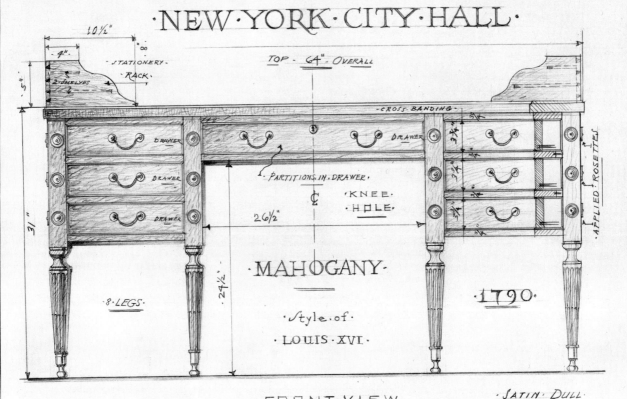

STATIONERY RACK

10½"

4"

8"

5"

2 SHELVES

TOP · 64" · OVERALL

CROSS-BANDING

DRAWER

DRAWER

DRAWER

DRAWER

PARTITIONS · IN · DRAWER

KNEE · HOLE

31"

26½"

24½"

8 · LEGS

MAHOGANY

Style · of
LOUIS · XVI

APPLIED · ROSETTES

1790

FRONT · VIEW

SATIN · DULL
FINISH

Note · BACK · VIEW · IS
SAME · AS · FRONT
FALSE · DETAILS
64" TOP

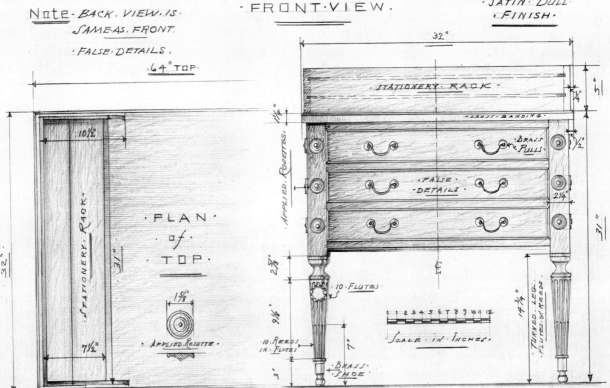

10½"

32"

STATIONERY · RACK

31"

7½"

PLAN
of
TOP

1⅝

APPLIED · ROSETTE

THE · PLAN

32"

STATIONERY · RACK

CROSS-BANDING

APPLIED · ROSETTES

BRASS
PULLS

FALSE
DETAILS

5"

4"

1½

2¼

31"

1¼

2⅞

9⅝

10 · FLUTES

10 · REEDS
IN · FLUTES

7"

0 1 2 3 4 5 6 7 8 9 10 11 12

SCALE · IN · INCHES

14¾"

TURNED · LEG
FLUTES & REEDS

3"

BRASS
SHOE

END · VIEW

Measured · & · Drawn · by · Lester Margon

GEORGE WASHINGTON'S DESK

Courtesy of Art Commission of the City of New York

By special courtesy of the Art Commission of the City of New York, we have the pleasure of including this desk used by George Washington in this volume of *American Furniture Treasures*. It is on view in the Governors' Room in the New York City Hall. On the top of the desk is the inscription – "Washington's Writing Table, 1789-1790." This was the period when Federal Hall in New York City was the capitol of the United States. The desk is made of mahogany in an adaptation of the style of Louis XVI. The design of the desk is unusual because the drawer divisions and the series of applied rosettes are carried out on all four sides. Of course, the treatment of the ends and the back is false. On the top are set two stationery compartments. Whereas their practical use is questionable, they do break the top surface advantageously. Besides the historical associations, this desk is of such a practical size that it could well be adapted for use in offices as well as in the home. The mahogany is straight-grained but the front edge of the top is cross-banded, producing a richness of effect. The interiors of the upper drawers are divided for stationery storage. Note that the legs have brass finials. The hardware is of the period and the desk does present a distinguished example of the cabinet-work of the times.

27

Photograph by Al Lichtenberg

The Henry Francis du Pont Winterthur Museum

The Henry Francis du Pont Winterthur Museum contains a collection of American decorative arts spanning the two hundred years from the 17th century through the early 19th century. In a great country house surrounded by a private park of striking beauty, are examples of domestic architecture, furniture, textiles, silver, pewter, ceramics, paintings and prints, shown in almost two hundred period rooms and special displays. All the furniture, with rare exceptions, was made in Colonial America. There are examples also made during the first years of the young Republic. The museum contains over 200 period rooms covering the early American domestic scene: drawing rooms, parlors, dining rooms, bedrooms, and simulated outdoor settings, each complete to the finest detail. There are morning and afternoon tours scheduled at the museum when visitors may inspect the collections. Reservations should be made in advance. For the casual visitor no appointment is needed to see the ten period rooms of the Reception Area, which are arranged chronologically to show the development of architectural and furniture styles from 1684 to 1840. There are also special exhibits. For the first time we have the privilege and the pleasure of including photographs from Winterthur in this volume. This will give a good idea of its complexity and distinction.

MORAVIAN ARMCHAIR

Philadelphia Museum of Art

This armchair in walnut is of Pennsylvania German origin, *circa* 1757-1760. This Moravian type wainscot chair was named after a group of settlers from Moravia belonging to a Protestant sect, who came to Pennsylvania and founded the city of Bethlehem. This chair is a most common type that was made in Germany and Switzerland. The chair is simple in design and well made. The shaped back splat is interesting if a bit formidable. The framing is sturdy. The curve of the arms is ingratiating, providing additional seating comfort. Of course, an upholstered knife cushion was always used with these chairs for comfort. For such an early date the use of walnut is unusual. Probably it was available. The armchair is stately and no doubt was used for special occasions, for it appears too foreboding for general use. The Pennsylvania Germans were prone to austerity in their furniture designs.

DESK·CHEST·OF·DRAWERS·
·FINE·ARTS·GALLERY·OF·SAN·DIEGO·

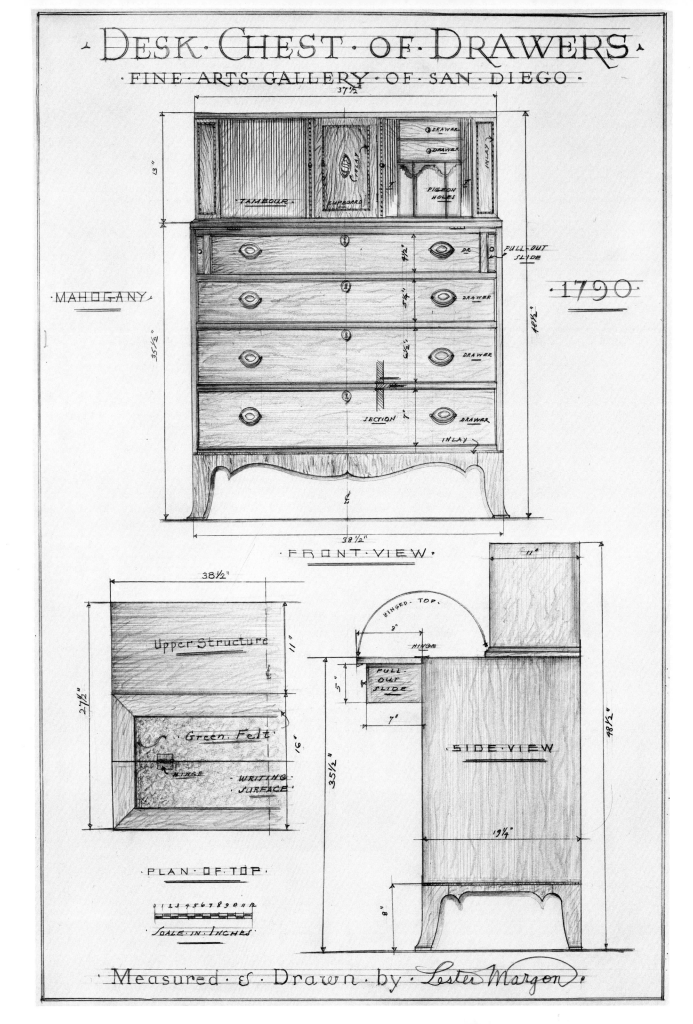

·MAHOGANY·

·1790·

·FRONT·VIEW·

·PLAN·OF·TOP·

0 1 2 3 4 5 6 7 8 9 10 11 12
·SCALE·IN·INCHES·

·SIDE·VIEW·

·Measured·&·Drawn·by·Lester Margon·

CHEST OF DRAWERS WITH DESK

The Fine Arts Gallery, San Diego   Gift of Mrs. Rowland Freeman

This elegant chest of drawers with a desk compartment, *circa* 1790, is in the style of George Hepplewhite. It is made of selected mahogany with inlays of satinwood and ebony. There are four drawers of varied sizes. The double fold-out top when opened provides an adequate writing surface, which has a panel of green felt. The mahogany is richly figured and there are contrasting bands of inlay. The chest is pleasing and in the best American tradition. Note that there are two tambour cupboards in the desk compartment enclosing drawers and pigeon-holes. A tambour is a sliding door made up of narrow strips of wood that are fastened to a backing of a heavy fabric. The doors slide in metal grooves at the top and bottom. The beauty and utility of such a chest lends itself for use in most any room in the house. Note that the encompassing bead around the drawer fronts is attached to the drawers. The pulls and escutcheon plates are of silver, of the period. While the inspiration of this piece is definitely English, the interpretation is definitely American. It is perhaps finer than its English predecessor. At least let us believe so. The piece is in the collection of the Fine Arts Gallery, Balboa Park, San Diego, California.

TAMBOUR DESK

The Henry Francis du Pont Winterthur Museum

This tambour desk of mahogany with satinwood inlays is labelled by John Seymour and Son of Creek Lane, Boston, *circa* 1795-1800. Seymour came from England and probably learned his craft there. He is considered one of the foremost cabinetmakers after the Revolution. His son, Thomas, was associated with him in business. The interior of this tambour desk is painted a curious robin's-egg blue. Other features of Seymour's work included inlaid pilasters, festoons, borders and lining. All of his furniture showed delicate proportions and splendid workmanship. It is easy to detect a piece of furniture attributed to John Seymour because there is always something erratic about it. There are many pieces made by him in the M. and M. Karolik Collection of the Boston Museum of Fine Arts. This particular tambour desk is in the collection of the Henry Francis du Pont Winterthur Museum.

TAMBOUR DESK CHEST

The Wadsworth Atheneum, Hartford

This mahogany Hepplewhite desk chest was made *circa* 1800. It probably hails from Massachusetts. Its simple dignity and ultra-refinement make it a significant piece of urban cabinetmaking. On the top of the desk compartment is a desk enclosed in a tambour front. The hinged top of the chest when opened creates an adequate writing surface. There are pull-outs at the sides to support this top when opened. Although rather sober in appearance, this desk chest is highly attractive and utilitarian, performing its various functions amicably. The interior of the desk compartment is filled with varied sized drawers, pigeon-holes and open spaces. It is a piece that would be appreciated in any home office by the man in the house. This tambour chest differs from the one from the Fine Arts Gallery in San Diego and is shown here for comparison. The piece is in the collection of the Wadsworth Atheneum in Hartford, Connecticut.

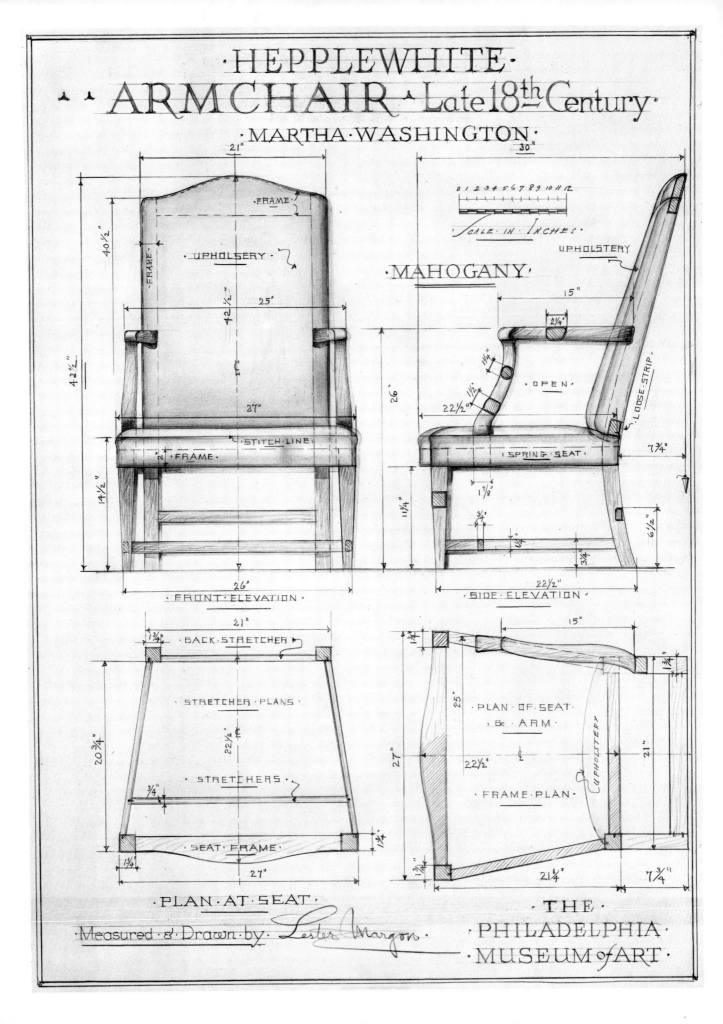

·HEPPLEWHITE·
·ARMCHAIR· Late 18th Century·
·MARTHA·WASHINGTON·

·MAHOGANY·

0 1 2 3 4 5 6 7 8 9 10 11 12
·Scale·in·Inches·

·FRONT·ELEVATION·

·SIDE·ELEVATION·

·PLAN·AT·SEAT·

·FRAME·PLAN·

·PLAN·OF·SEAT· &· ARM·

Measured & Drawn by Lester Margon·

·THE·
·PHILADELPHIA·
·MUSEUM of ART·

HEPPLEWHITE ARMCHAIR
Philadelphia Museum of Art

This very gracious mahogany armchair is in the Hepplewhite tradition of the late 18th century. It is known that Martha Washington had several of this type of chair in Mt. Vernon. She was partial to them. The reason for this favor may be the chair's unpretentious appearance and the excellent seating comfort. This is probably the most popular living room chair that has ever been made and its popularity has continued to this day. For the modest home it can be upholstered in ordinary material. For the more pretentious interior the upholstery can be of the richest fabric. The graceful shaped arm, the simple tapered leg and the straight stretchers give this chair strength and durability. The high back is impressive and the curved front of the seat is gracious. One could go far to find a better chair for ordinary use in the living room. The style is simple and direct and permits of no procrastination. The construction of this chair is simple and firm and will outlast many a more fanciful seating piece. After all, what is the purpose of a living room chair but to provide comfort and affability? The Philadelphia Museum of Art is happy to have a model of this chair in the collection.

WHITBY HALL – DRAWING ROOM

Detroit Institute of Arts

Whitby Hall was one of the finest examples of Georgian architecture in Colonial America. In 1927, when the growth of Philadelphia threatened its existence, the Detroit Institute of Arts took several of the interiors and incorporated them in a new wing. In the days of its prime, Whitby Hall was the center of social and political life. Colonel Coultas moved into the house in 1741 and enlarged it in 1754. The drawing room does not contain the original furniture. The Museum has selected Chippendale, Hepplewhite and Sheraton furniture to replace it. The fine winged fireside chair is in the Queen Anne style. The superb low-boy has elaborately carved cabriole legs with ball-and-claw feet. A finely carved shell is carved into the lower central drawer. The elegant mirror above is also of the Chippendale style, *circa* 1761. The drapes are toiles de Jouy. Whitby Hall was "Built in the Old Colonial day / When men lived in a grander way / With ampler hospitality."

SHERATON ARMCHAIR

Museum of Fine Arts, Boston   M. and M. Karolik Collection

One of a pair, this Sheraton armchair in mahogany from Boston, *circa* 1795, is attributed to John Seymour. He is considered the foremost designer and craftsman after the Revolution. All of his furniture shows fine workmanship and splendid proportions. The excellence of his carving is paramount. The great M. and M. Karolik Collection at the Museum of Fine Arts in Boston is fortunate in having quite a few of his pieces including a tambour sideboard, a Hepplewhite secretary and this elegant armchair. The juxtaposition of the mahogany and the upholstery is masterfully handled. Chairs of this quality are rare and highly prized by museums and collectors. In the Haverhill House of the American Wing of the Metropolitan Museum of Art in New York, there is a mahogany bed with richly carved posts attributed to John Seymour. Many of his pieces combined mahogany with satinwood with dazzling effect.

37

Mahogany & Satinwood CHEST of DRAWERS

ART·INSTITUTE·OF·CHICAGO·

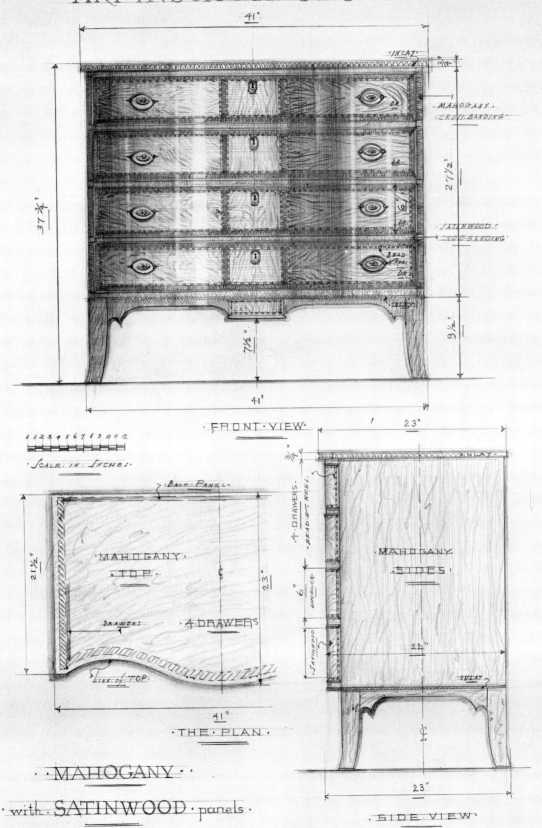

FRONT·VIEW

·SCALE·IN·INCHES·

·THE·PLAN·

·MAHOGANY·

with SATINWOOD panels·

SIDE·VIEW

·Measured & Drawn by· Lester Margon·

MAHOGANY AND SATINWOOD CHEST OF DRAWERS

Art Institute of Chicago   Gift of the Antiquarian Society

This Hepplewhite mahogany and satinwood chest of drawers, *circa* 1790-1810, is from Salem, Massachusetts. It is one of the grandest examples of a four-drawer satinwood panelled front chest. The quality is superb. It may be considered a masterpiece of cabinet-work. It is another original product of which America can be proud. The combination of mahogany and satinwood is always exciting. The graceful serpentine plan of the front produces the opportunity for spectacular play of light and shade enhanced by the miraculous markings of the crotch satinwood. Note that all the dividing members are cross-banded as well as all the borders around the drawers. As though this were not enough, a carved bead and reel moulding has been added on the inside of the drawer borders. The brass pulls and escutcheon plates are jewel-like and of the period. They are dramatically placed. This is one of the rare pieces that is purely American and for which there is no peer. It is perfection exemplified. To come across such a brilliant performance is indeed a joy. The chest of drawers is one of the treasures in the furniture collection of the Art Institute of Chicago.

HEPPLEWHITE BREAKFRONT

The Henry Francis du Pont Winterthur Museum

This mahogany breakfront is one of the handsomest pieces of furniture that was made, *circa* 1775, in Massachusetts. While it certainly is in the Hepplewhite style it contains heraldings of the approaching Federal period. The lower section contains a desk compartment with a drop front. At the sides are two drawers and two large cupboards. The upper bookcase section has four glass doors protected by complicated mahogany grills outlined in satinwood. The cornice is refined, with a shaped top piece. There are five turned brass finials, the center one being capped by a cast eagle, so emblematic of the times. The features of this elegant breakfront are the satinwood and ebony inlay, the multiple borders and the inlaid panels. The crotch wood, so well selected, is used to the utmost effectiveness. Truly there is nothing finer than these great breakfronts in the field of cabinetmaking. They are refined, elegant and distinctive, possessing a regality that is unsurpassed. This breakfront is in the collection of the Henry Francis du Pont Winterthur Museum.

PAINTED SIDE CHAIR

The Brooklyn Museum   Bequest of Mrs. William Sterling Peters

This "fancy" side chair is painted black with colorful painted decoration and gold stencilling. Designated as the Empire Style, American, *circa* 1825-1835, it is really a variation of the popular Lambert Hitchcock chair designs. The swans shown on the top back rail seem to be drinking from a flowing fountain surrounded by leaf groupings. There is a definite Pompeiian flavor to the decoration, all in the Classical style. The caned shaped seat is typical. The chair is elegant and produces the impression of regality. These "fancy" chairs of the period are so interesting because they break away from tradition and create a new world of undiscovered imagery. They are unique and different and encourage new approaches to furniture and especially to chair design.

LOWBOY · Massachusetts · 1720

The · M. H. De Young · Memorial · Museum

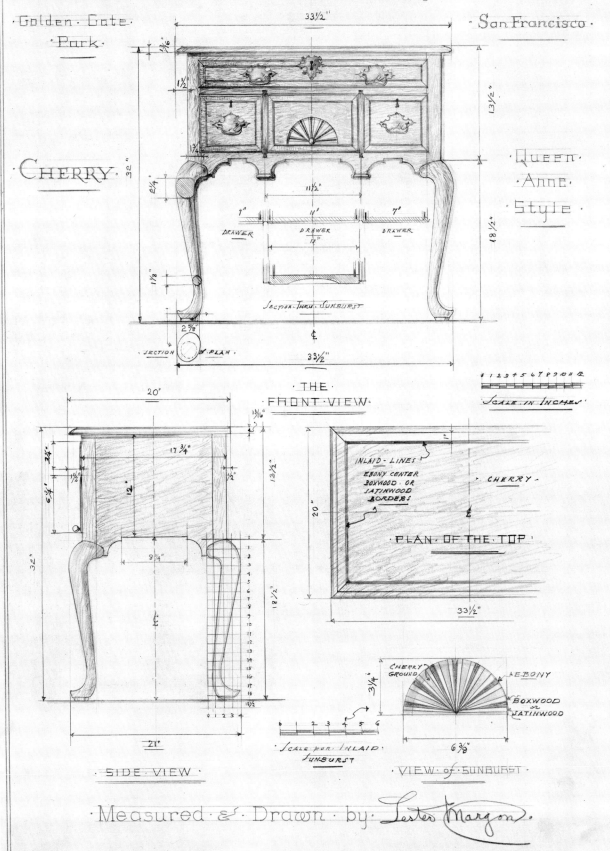

Golden · Gate · Park

San Francisco

CHERRY

Queen · Anne · Style

33½"

3/16"

1½"

13½"

1¾"

32"

2¼"

18½"

1⅛"

11½"

7'   11'   7'

DRAWER   DRAWER   DRAWER

4"

SECTION · THRU · SUNBURST

2⅞"

SECTION & PLAN

℄

33½"

THE FRONT VIEW

1 2 3 4 5 6 7 8 9 10 11 12
SCALE IN INCHES

20"

13/16"

¾"

17¾"

1½"

½"

6½"

2"

13½"

32"

8¼"

18½"

0 1 2 3
1 2 3 4 5 6 7 8 9 10 11 12 13 14 15 16 17 18 18½

21"

SIDE VIEW

INLAID · LINES

EBONY CENTER
BOXWOOD · OR ·
SATINWOOD
BORDERS

· CHERRY ·

20"

℄

PLAN · OF · THE · TOP

33½"

CHERRY
GROUND

·EBONY

BOXWOOD
or
SATINWOOD

3¾"

6⅜"

0 1 2 3 4 5 6
SCALE FOR INLAID
SUNBURST

VIEW · of · SUNBURST

Measured · & · Drawn · by · Lester Margon.

MASSACHUSETTS LOWBOY

M. H. de Young Memorial Museum   Gift of the Estate of Mrs. Julia Dunn

Lowboys of this character were usually made of walnut or mahogany, but this one is an exception. The wood used was cherry. The locale is Massachusetts and the date *circa* 1720. The style is definitely Queen Anne. Usually the decoration on these high- and lowboys consisted of carved shell motifs, but in this instance the designer chose to insert a radiating semi-circle of ebony, cherry and satinwood. This makes the lowboy individual and distinctive. The broken line of the apron is unadorned. Usually acorn pendants are applied to the two dropped divisions. Again, this makes this model a bit unusual. Of particular interest are the cabriole legs, whose violent slope with the decisive curve at the base is refreshing. There is one long drawer at the top and three smaller drawers below. The hardware is elegant. Note also the simple inlaid line border on the top, of ebony and satinwood. This lowboy could only have been used as a side table as there is not adequate height for seating before it. By reason of its simplicity and good space divisions, this lowboy could grace the finest hall or living room. It is such a relief to find such a lowboy of this date, that does not follow the prescribed rules and regulations.

43

WALNUT LOWBOY
Philadelphia Museum of Art

This William and Mary lowboy in walnut, *circa* 1700, is a typical example of the period. The features are an inlaid top with a wide border of crossbanding and narrower borders of matched herringbone. The trumpet legs are exemplary, held in place by a shaped crossed stretcher which is supported by bun feet. The apron is discreetly shaped, with acorn pendants. The dropped pulls are of brass, originals, correct in design. So much for the data concerning this lowboy. What makes it so unusual and distinctive is the unique oriental character which it holds. There are so many lowboys of this type but this one is different and unique.

It may be used as a desk or a vanity with a mirror hung above. What could be finer than placing it in a foyer to serve as a console table? Pieces of this type can be used in most any room in the house with elegant effect. The Philadelphia Museum of Art has so many fabulous treasures but this lowboy seemed particularly pleasing. The origin of the lowboy is obscure. Many writers have different notions, but perhaps the most logical solution is that the lowboy is a development of the table which has been augmented with period characteristics. It is certainly one of the most decorative pieces of furniture design.

44

CURLY MAPLE LOWBOY

Museum of Fine Arts, Boston

This Queen Anne curly maple lowboy, *circa* 1720-1750, is of the Goddard-Townsend vintage from Newport, Rhode Island. The design is conventional, but this lowboy is unique by reason of the curious hump at the knee of the cabriole leg and the fluting at the foot. The shaped apron provides the placing of two pendant drops which do not quite reveal the usual acorn shaping. The carved sunburst in the center lower drawer is incised to heighten the effect. There are two small drawers near the top and three larger drawers below. The tiger-stripe of the maple veneer adds much to the attractiveness of the lowboy. This piece is in the collection of the Museum of Fine Arts in Boston.

BLOCK·FRONT·CHEST·of·DRAWERS

·MUSEUM·OF·FINE·ARTS·BOSTON·

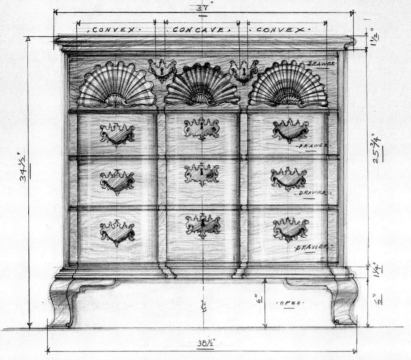

·CONVEX· ·CONCAVE· ·CONVEX·

37"

1½"

34½"

25¾"

DRAWER

DRAWER

DRAWER

1¼"

6"

OPEN

5"

38½"

· FRONT·VIEW ·

0 1 2 3 4 5 6 7 8 9 10 11 12

· Scale·in·Inches ·

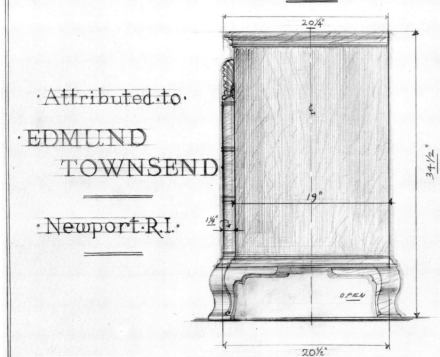

20¼"

· Attributed·to·

EDMUND
TOWNSEND

· Newport·R.I. ·

34½"

19"

1½"

OPEN

20½"

· MAHOGANY·

· Circa ·

· 1760-1770 ·

· SIDE·VIEW ·

· Measured· &·Drawn· by· Lester Margon ·

BLOCK-FRONT CHEST OF DRAWERS

Museum of Fine Arts, Boston   The M. and M. Karolik Collection

This block-front chest of drawers in mahogany is attributed to Edmund Townsend of Newport, Rhode Island, *circa* 1760-1770. This piece is remarkable in scope, strength and superb execution. The block front of the drawers was cut from a solid piece of mahogany and glued to the face. The top drawer is enhanced by two convex shell carvings. In the center is a carved concave shell carving. This affords the proper amount of contrast. The brass pulls and escutcheon plates are extraordinary as is fitting on such a splendid piece

of cabinetmaking. Chestnut is the secondary wood used and the drawer interiors are made of white wood. All the features of this chest, the raised bead around the drawers, the ogee bracket feet, the excellent top and bottom mouldings, all form an harmonious entity. Every detail seems to have been carefully planned and expertly executed. This is another American piece that is completely original in design. It is in the collection of the Museum of Fine Arts, Boston, a part of the famous M. and M. Karolik assemblage.

DROP-FRONT DESK

The Henry Francis du Pont Winterthur Museum

This maple desk is attributed to a member of the Dunlap family of Chester and Salisbury, New Hampshire, *circa* 1770-1790. Of unique interest in this piece is the unusually large intaglio carved fan on the lower center drawer front. There are other bits of character carving. The bracket feet are attached to a weird scroll form which continues across the front. There are three long drawers of varying sizes and four smaller drawers at the sides. The drop front discloses a series of drawers and pigeon holes. All furniture that is attributed to the Dunlap family is unorthodox, featuring a combination of scrolls, interlaced pediments and peculiar carving, and all of their pieces have a low center of gravity. These pieces are easily identified by reason of their individuality. This desk is in the collection at the Henry Francis du Pont Winterthur Museum.

BLOCK-FRONT DESK

The Wadsworth Atheneum, Hartford, Connecticut

This elegant block-front Chippendale desk in mahogany is from New England, *circa* 1750-1780. When opened it reveals a gallery of drawers, cupboard and pigeon holes. The layout is superb. The lower chest of drawers is distinguished by the block front and the cabriole legs with the ball-and-claw feet. The brass pulls and escutcheon plates are most decorative. The straight-grained mahogany provides the proper austerity. All the details are well co-ordinated. It is a splendid example of this type of desk. There is a similar desk in the M. and M. Karolik collection in the Museum of Fine Arts in Boston. In the New York Historical Society Museum there is a similar desk on which George Washington signed the death warrant of Major André.

GEORGIAN · LOVE · SEAT

METROPOLITAN · MUSEUM · OF · ART

58"

1/4"

14"

10"

36 3/4"

UPHOLSTERY

SPRING · BACK

SPOOL

12 1/2"

38"

26 3/4"

SPRING · SEAT

MAHOGANY

8"

18 3/4"

6 3/4"

14 1/4"

BALL & CLAW

FRONT · VIEW

50"

SEAT · PLAN

BRACE

1750

12"

22 1/2"

BACK · UPHOLSTERY

BACK · POST

9 1/4"

SPOOL

WOOD · FRAME

CORNER · BLOCK

LOOSE · STRIP

SEAT · FRAME

4"

54 1/2"

CARVED · CABRIOLE · LEGS

14 1/4"

LEG · DETAILS

2 1/4"

1 7/8"

SECTIONS

1 9/16"

1 3/16"

0 1 2 3 4 5
SCALE · IN · INCHES

0 1 2 3 4 5 6 7 8 9 10 11 12
SCALE · IN · INCHES

26 1/2"

SIDE · VIEW

Measured & Drawn by Lester Margon

GEORGIAN LOVE SEAT

Metropolitan Museum of Art, New York   *Sylmaris Collection, Gift of Mrs. George Coe Graves, 1930*

A love seat is a most propitious piece of furniture that permits two persons to huddle together. In this instance, it is adequate in size, graceful in demeanor, with excellent seating potentialities. It is from the famous Sylmaris Collection and graces the halls of the Verplanck Room. Besides the green damask upholstery, the exemplary cabriole legs embody the salient characteristics of the best work of Thomas Chippendale. The making of a cabriole leg is possibly the most intriguing problem for the cabinetmaker. It has no prescribed rules or regulations. The lines must sing and the

rhythm needs to be perfect. It is the most sensitive involvement of his labors. Going from a block of wood at the seat down to a slender rounded section, only to expand into a ball-and-claw foot, the fashioning of a cabriole leg requires not alone the carver's skill but the involvement of heart and soul. It is like a melody that rings loud only to fade away in diminuendo. In this instance the wood is mahogany. The knee of the cabriole leg is profusely carved with acanthus enrichment. The date is 1750-1775.

CALDWALLADER COLDEN HOUSE
Metropolitan Museum of Art, New York

The woodwork in this room is from the Caldwallader Colden House in Coldenham, New York, *circa* 1767. The furnishings are from the Verplanck Drawing Room, New York, New York. The combination is excellent. The panelling of the room is Classical restrained, and the unobtrusive fireplace seems to fit into the scheme well. The furniture is Chippendale. The chairs are magnificent and the gaming table beyond compare. The original rug seems to hold things together. The japanned decorated bookcase and secretary adds just the needed touch of color. If perfection in a room is possible this surely is a fair example. It breathes of culture and opulence, exemplifying the period when life of the aristocracy proceeded with dignity and éclair.

52

PHILADELPHIA ARMCHAIR

The Henry Francis du Pont Winterthur Museum

This armchair, labeled Benjamin Randolph, is similar to a chair in the M. and M. Karolik Collection in Boston. The arms and the well-shaped arm supports are especially well defined. The chair is definitely of Chippendale inspiration for the pierced center splat and the curvatures of the top rail cannot be denied. The cabriole legs are a bit slender and the ball-and-claw feet are a little too well defined. The upholstery is cream-colored silk damask, French, of the early 18th century. Benjamin Randolph was born in Monmouth

County, New Jersey. His shop "The Golden Eagle" was situated on Chestnut Street. He used the plates of Chippendale for advertising purposes. The legend on the advertisements was "All sorts of Cabinet and Chair Work Made and Sold by Benj. Randolph." His furniture reveals him as one of the great cabinetmakers of America. There are examples in Williamsburg, Philadelphia, Boston and in the Garvin Collection at Yale University. This armchair may be seen at the Henry Francis du Pont Museum in Winterthur.

53

LIST OF ILLUSTRATIONS

(Asterisks indicate photographs accompanied by measured drawings.)

TULIP AND SUNFLOWER CHEST*
  Wadsworth Atheneum, Hartford
CUPBOARD OR "KAS"
  Art Institute of Chicago
OAK AND PINE CHEST
  Wadsworth Atheneum, Hartford
WINDOW BENCH*
  Museum of the City of New York
WHITBY HALL, NORTH BEDROOM
  Detroit Institute of Arts
PAINTED FANCY SIDE CHAIR
  Winterthur Museum
EARLY AMERICAN DOWER CHEST*
  Detroit Institute of Arts
BLANKET CHEST
  Wadsworth Atheneum, Hartford
DOWER CHEST
  Philadelphia Museum of Art
HANGING CABINET*
  Philadelphia Museum of Art
BREWSTER ARMCHAIR
  Metropolitan Museum of Art
HIGH CHEST ON A STAND
  Philadelphia Musem of Art

KITCHEN CABINET*
  Brooklyn Museum, New York
KITCHEN CUPBOARD
  Old Sturbridge Village
PAINTED CHEST OF DRAWERS
  Winterthur Museum
SLANT-TOP DESK AND BOOKCASE*
  Wadsworth Atheneum, Hartford
DESK AND BOOKCASE
  Colonial Willamsburg
DESK-BOOKCASE
  Heritage Foundation
LIBRARY TABLE*
  Wadsworth Atheneum, Hartford
SLANT-TOP DESK
  Wadsworth Atheneum, Hartford
PENNSYLVANIA GERMAN TABLE
  Philadelphia Museum of Art
FOLDING CARD TABLE*
  Museum of the City of New York
LOOKING-GLASS
  Winterthur Museum
DRESSING TABLE
  Heritage Foundation

OUR HERITAGE

THE response to the previous book, *Masterpieces of American Furniture*, proves that there is an insatiable interest in this furniture. Other styles may come and go, but the distinctive qualities of American furniture are our heritage: these pieces welcome us like old friends. This is furniture we know and understand.

Events and eras of our country's history are reflected in these pieces, styles of living in different regions, and each group of immigrants, many of them the poor, the oppressed, the seekers after greater religious liberty, adding their influence as they came to find a new home and a better life. They contributed by their suffering, hard work, and eventual success to our heritage.

It was here that the Shakers established their "Homes." Settling first near Waterliet, New York in 1774, they soon established settlements throughout the colonies. They were a people known for their industry and integrity, and their furniture reflected these qualities: it was based on traditional lines, but embodied simplicity of design and excellent construction. A feature of Shaker wall cabinets was manifold drawers, "to provide space for everything."

The Shakers honored the counsel of their leader, Mother Ann Lee, "Do all your work as though you had a thousand years to live, and as you would if you knew you must die tomorrow." The cause of the eventual demise of the Shakers was, however, the provision of celibacy in their "Rules of Conduct." Their way of life was summarized in the words "Hands to work and hearts to God."

William Penn encouraged German colonists from the Rhineland to immigrate to this country. They arrived in Pennsylvania in 1683, settling in Germantown near Philadelphia. The promise of freedom of worship and the grants of fertile lands were most attractive. These people were largely farmers, though there was a sprinkling of artisans among them. This influx from the Rhine valley brought a distinctive cultural contribution to Colonial life.

The Germans were governed by rules and regulations particular to themselves. These restrictions hold good to this day in Mennonite communities. The same horse-drawn buggies, black with shielded sides, are evident everywhere. Mennonite furniture reflected the homeland, incorporating symbols — hearts, tulips, unicorns, and cherubs — in their decoration. The Mennonites built huge two-door cupboards often fabulously decorated with scenes from the scriptures.

So it was with many other peoples and cults. There were the rich burghers in New York, the militant French Huguenots, the petulant English, the Scandinavian peasants, and the persistent Irish. Many people of the Jewish faith from Central Europe came to this country in search of a more rewarding life. Our melting pot has created a great nation of diverse peoples. This book shows the different styles of furniture that have developed in this country, contributions which all of us, from our different backgrounds, can share and appreciate together.

TULIP & SUNFLOWER CHEST

· WADSWORTH · ATHENEUM · HARTFORD ·

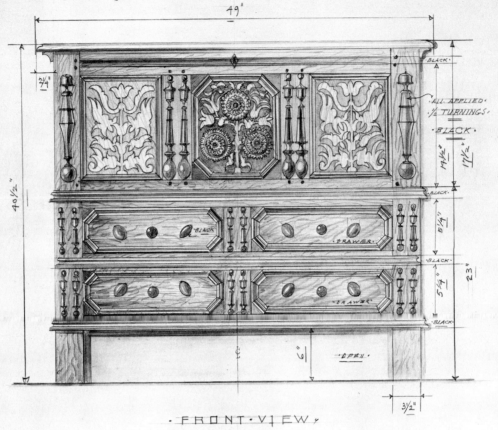

· FRONT · VIEW ·

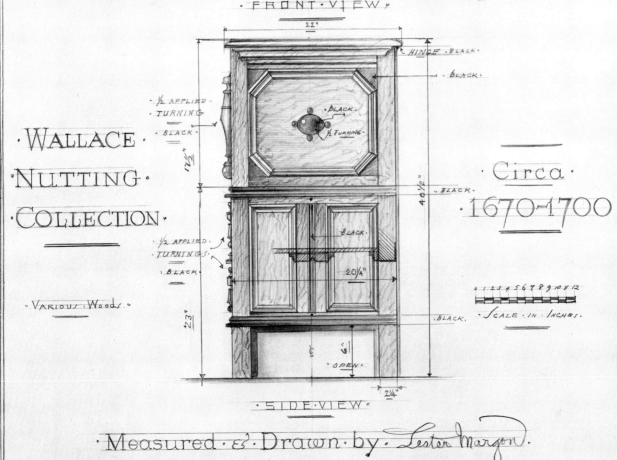

· WALLACE ·

· NUTTING ·

· COLLECTION ·

· VARIOUS WOODS ·

· Circa ·
1670-1700

· SCALE · IN · INCHES ·

· SIDE · VIEW ·

Measured & Drawn by Lester Margon

TULIP AND SUNFLOWER CHEST

Wadsworth Atheneum, Hartford   Gift of J. P. Morgan, Wallace Nutting Collection

This tulip and sunflower chest over drawers, *circa* 1670-1700, is from the Hartford-Wethersfield area. It is made of oak, maple and pine. Purely American in character, it is one of the finest contributions to Early American furniture design. The carving is articulate and deep. The bold split applied turnings are ebonized to provide the necessary contrast. The dividing mouldings are also black. This gives the character and distinction to the chest. It is part of the vast Wallace Nutting Collection, the gift of J. P. Morgan to the Wadsworth Atheneum in Hartford, Connecticut. There

has been so much talk about how American furniture was fashioned after English models that it is a pleasure to find some pieces that are entirely original. This chest is one. Many of these chests were made in Connecticut but this particular one is from the Hartford area and is therefore doubly interesting. The tulip was the Colonial flower but the sunflower goes with it so well as the central motif of the chest. There are two long drawers below divided by moulded panels. The bosses and the turned wooden knobs are also ebonized.

CUPBOARD OR "KAS"

Art Institute of Chicago   Decorative Arts Fund

This oak cupboard or "kas" is from the Hudson Valley or possibly New Jersey, *circa* late 17th century. This is a typical American interpretation of the Jacobean style with the applied shaped bosses set on raised panels. There are two large doors enclosing shelves and two small drawers below. The protruding cornice conceals two additional secret drawers. This massive cupboard is supported by turned bun feet. The piece is almost square, measuring 67″ wide x 66″ high. Despite its crudity, the cupboard is impressive by reason of the clever treatment of light and shade. These cupboards were often set in kitchens to hold the culinary objects. In Colonial times the kitchen was the main place of assemblage for the family.

OAK AND PINE CHEST

Wadsworth Atheneum, Hartford   *The Wallace Nutting Collection*

This Jacobean chest of drawers is made of oak but the bottom, back and the interior construction are pine. The date 1760 is about as early as any pieces of Colonial furniture have survived. The front shows varied size drawers which are decorated with a series of applied mouldings. The large second drawer and the lowest drawer have additional applied panels. Note that the legs are an extension of the corner posts. The extended top and the moulding at the base serve as definite beginning and ending. The mouldings between the drawers continue right across the face of the chest. This piece is in the Wallace Nutting Col-

lection of the Wadsworth Atheneum. The sides of the chest have panels which continue right to the corner posts. Chests of this period were made in the vicinity of Connecticut. Many of them were much more elaborate, with applied half-turnings and carving. While most of the furniture at this time followed the European prototypes, the Colonial cabinetmakers introduced new factors that had a native appeal. When looking at this type of chest one gets a feeling of seeing a rich tapestry. The all-over decoration is most effective. There is something about the use of oak that brings back the spirit of the Middle Ages.

BENCH Attributed to D. PHYFE
MUSEUM OF THE CITY OF NEW YORK

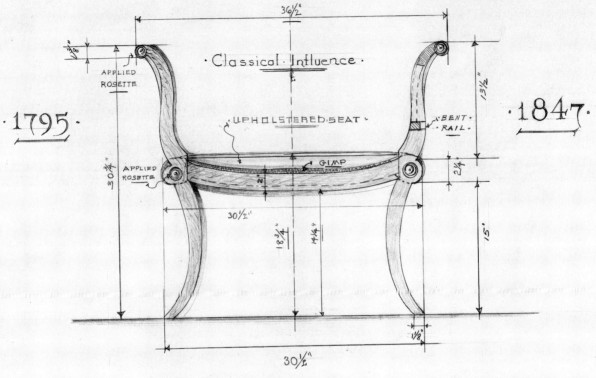

· 1795 ·   · 1847 ·

· Classical Influence ·

UPHOLSTERED SEAT

GIMP

BENT RAIL

APPLIED ROSETTE

APPLIED ROSETTE

36½"   13½"   2¼"   15"   30½"   18¾"   14¼"   1⅛"   ⅛"

· FRONT · VIEW ·
· OF · BENCH ·

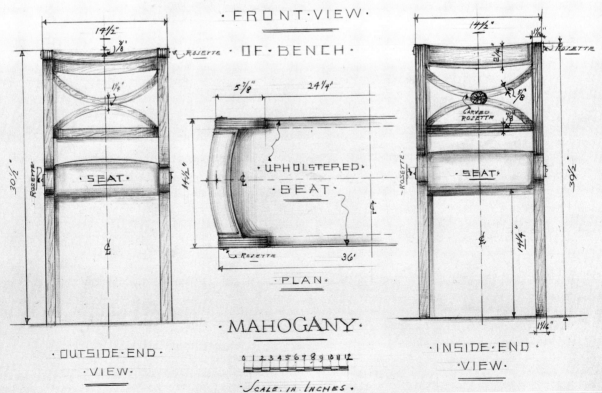

ROSETTE

SEAT

· OUTSIDE · END ·
· VIEW ·

5⅞"   24¼"

UPHOLSTERED
SEAT

ROSETTE   36"

· PLAN ·

· MAHOGANY ·

0 1 2 3 4 5 6 7 8 9 10 11 12

· SCALE · IN · INCHES ·

ROSETTE

CARVED
ROSETTE

SEAT

· INSIDE · END ·
· VIEW ·

14½"   30½"   14½"   39½"   14¼"   1⁵⁄₁₆"

· Measured · & · Drawn · by · Lester Margon ·

WINDOW BENCH

Museum of the City of New York   The Gift of Miss Adelaide de Groot

The Museum of the City of New York at 103rd Street facing Central Park, is the proud owner of this window seat, one of a pair, by Duncan Phyfe. It is made of mahogany with a fitted upholstered seat. The two curved sides are supported by a graceful double curved fret which is held in place by a carved rosette. There is a magnificent rhythm in this bench that reflects the supreme artistry of one of America's foremost designers and cabinet-makers. Duncan Phyfe's name is associated with the making of chairs, window seats, sofas, sewing tables, settees and sideboards. He employed over a hundred journeymen but all the work was done under his personal supervision. He was the most favored cabinetmaker of his time and clients paid well for his products. The amount of work pro-duced in his shops during fifty-five years is enor-mous. However, many pieces attributed to him have no verification and should come under the heading of the School of Duncan Phyfe. One fea-ture of his work was acanthus carving which was expertly executed in fine detail. In chairs, of which he was a master, he showed definite Shera-ton influence but the Directoire trend was ap-parent. Of course, the lyre back was his favor-ite, which he made in various interpretations. Later in his career, the French Empire style pre-vailed. He tried his hand at this style but was not very successful. A fine collection of his furniture may be seen at the Henry Ford Museum in Dear-born, Michigan, as well as in many other collec-tions throughout the country.

63

WHITBY HALL — NORTH BEDROOM

Detroit Institute of Arts

The North Bedroom of Whitby Hall, originally located above the Drawing Room, is rather sophisticated in its furnishings. It contains a Sheraton type four-poster bed on a dais. The bed is festooned with the original 18th century toile de Jouy hangings depicting Indians shooting at a fort. Near the bed (not shown) stands a Queen Anne tea table and there are several sewing tables about, with sewing bags of French silk. In these the mistress kept her yarn and sewing paraphernalia.

There is the inevitable winged easy chair covered in the original 17th century brocatelle. A Martha Washington armchair stands unobtrusively in the corner. Facing the bed is a bombé chest of drawers with strong Dutch influence. There are several ribbon-back Chippendale side chairs. The room panelling is simple, emphasizing the dignity and good taste of Colonial America. The fireplace is faced with Carrara marble. In the hearth are tall andirons holding the resting logs.

PAINTED "FANCY" SIDE CHAIR

The Henry Francis du Pont Winterthur Museum

This painted "fancy" chair is made of tulip and other woods. It is one of a set probably made in New York, *circa* 1810. It was thought to have come from the Van Rensselaer family manor house at Albany, New York. The wide center splat shows an idyllic scene of the Hudson River, a favorite romantic subject of the period, popularized by the stories of Washington Irving and the invention of the steamboat by Robert Fulton.

The term "fancy" chair is in no way degrading. It simply means that it is away from the ordinary and conventional type of chair. This side chair, for instance, is most decorative and pleasing. The rounded caned seat, the unusual turned and carved legs that point outwards and the entire design is so well organized that it surpasses by far many conventional chairs. This model is in the Henry Francis du Pont Winterthur Museum.

EARLY·AMERICAN·DOWER·CHEST·

·DETROIT·INSTITUTE·OF·ARTS·

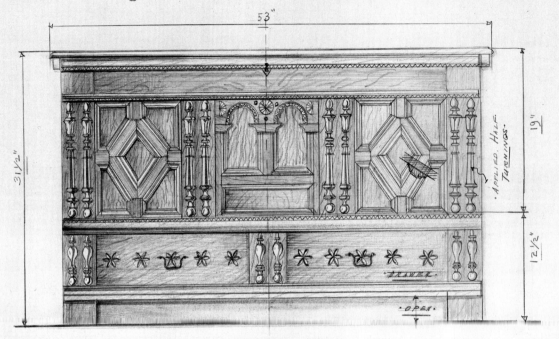

53"

31½"

19"

·APPLIED·HALF· TURNINGS·

12½"

DRAWER

·OPEN·

·FRONT·VIEW·

·OAK·

&

·PINE·

1 2 3 4 5 6 7 8 9 10 11 12
·SCALE·IN·INCHES·

·Circa·1690·

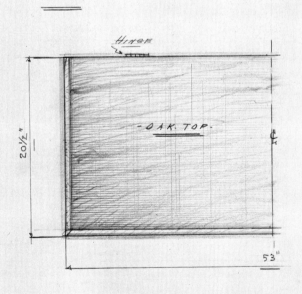

HINGE

20½"

·OAK·TOP·

53"

·TOP·PLAN·

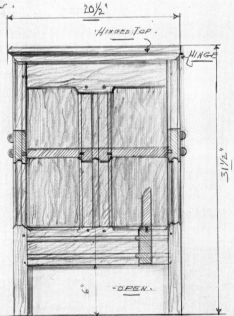

20½"

·HINGED·TOP·

HINGE

31½"

6"

·OPEN·

·END·VIEW·

·Measured·&·Drawn·by· Lester Margon·

EARLY AMERICAN DOWER CHEST
Detroit Institute of Arts

In the Pilgrim Century dower chests were the cherished possession of every maiden. They were often most elaborate, being decorated on all four sides so the piece might stand in the center of the room. This Early American dower chest, *circa* 1690, is made of oak and pine. The chest is painted with the structural members in a pine green and the panels in brown. The design is Tudor. It is delightful and quite sophisticated for this early date. These chests were meticulously made, with painstaking care, as was appropriate for these labors of love. There is one long drawer at the bottom and the hinged top, when lifted, probably disclosed a lift-out tray for the smaller accessories. The dower chests of Berks County were different. They were painted and profusely decorated with turtle-doves, tulips, unicorns and cavaliers on their way to plead their case for the hand of the lovely maiden. These chests were the repositories for the maiden's treasured possessions and exemplified her perfect trust in her life's eventual fulfillment in the sanctity of marriage. What dreams of future love and happiness evolved from these chests.

BLANKET CHEST

Wadsworth Atheneum, Hartford   *The Wallace Nutting Collection, Gift of J. P. Morgan, Jr.*

This serrated blanket chest in oak, *circa* 1691, is typical of the best work of the Pilgrim Century. The matching of the three geometrical panels is exceptional, divided by the bold split turnings. The dividing mouldings are carved. There are two drawers below. Many of these chests were placed before the beds to hold blankets, which was made possible by the hinged top. This chest was probably made in Massachusetts. Much of its beauty depends upon the lusty grain of the wood and the way it is placed. This chest is in the Wallace Nutting Collection given to the Wadsworth Atheneum in Hartford, Connecticut, by J. P. Morgan, Jr. Wallace Nutting had a way of getting around and picking up thousands of country antiques. Some of them were not so good but others were paramount.

DOWER CHEST

Philadelphia Museum of Art

This Pennsylvania German dower chest of painted pine is dated *circa* 1788. It has ogee bracket feet and the two lower drawers with overlapping edges are separated by the sunken background. The top is hinged, affording ample space for storage. No doubt there is a lift-out tray included. The painted chest, in this instance, is decorated on all four sides. The design is worked out in a compass technique, achieving the effect of precise hearts and tulips. The design is divided into panels by vertical ornaments and the date is inscribed below the escutcheon plate. These dower chests were labors of love and finished in every detail with awareness and skill. Every maiden had a dower chest and regarded it as a symbol of her future happiness. This chest is in the collection of the Philadelphia Museum of Art.

HANGING · CABINET · PHILADELPHIA

MUSEUM · OF · ART ·

· Pennsylvania · German · 1750 ·

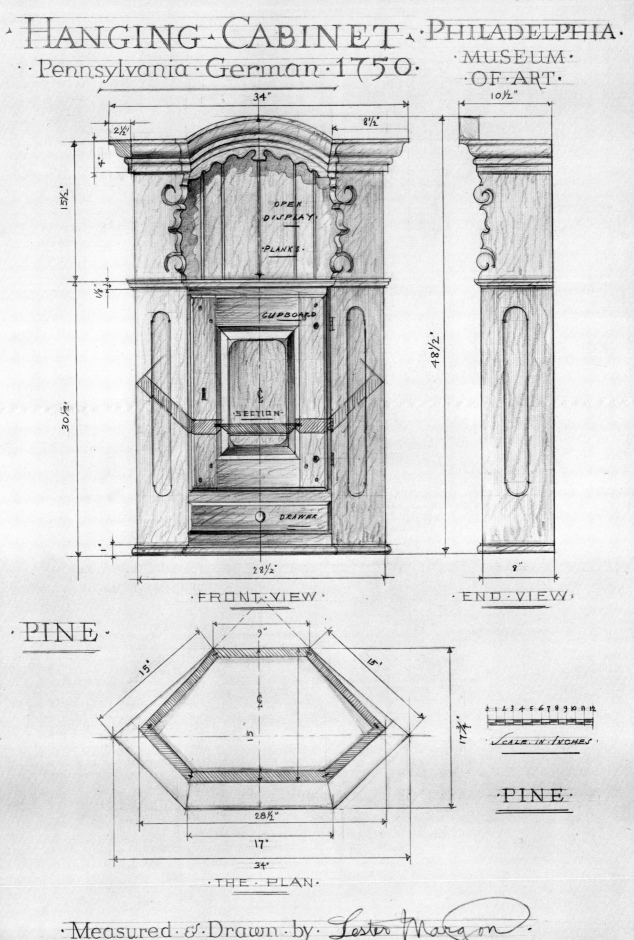

34"

8½"

2½"

4"

15½"

10½"

OPEN
DISPLAY
PLANKS

1⅛"

48½"

CUPBOARD

30½"

SECTION

DRAWER

1"

28½"

· FRONT · VIEW ·

· END · VIEW ·

8"

· PINE ·

9"

15"

15"

17¾"

C

5"

0 1 2 3 4 5 6 7 8 9 10 11 12
· SCALE · IN · INCHES ·

28½"

17"

· PINE ·

34"

· THE · PLAN ·

· Measured · & · Drawn · by · Lester Margon ·

HANGING CABINET
Philadelphia Museum of Art

This Pennsylvania German hanging cabinet is made of pine, dating from *circa* 1750. This piece is typical of the furniture made by the settlers who sought freedom from religious persecution, in America. The cabinet is simple, sturdy, well-balanced and straightforward. It is just what it was intended to be, a hanging corner cabinet with one door opening to a large storage area, and a small drawer below. Above is a scalloped open space for the display of a treasured piece of majolica brought over from the *Vaterland*. In the Philadelphia Museum of Art is a group of rooms reset from the House of the Miller of Millbach, Lebanon County, Pennsylvania, 1752. With its great fireplace, this affords a propitious setting for this type of furniture. The cornice at the top gives the cabinet the proper virility. The plan is engaging, producing the effect of fitting right into a corner. The use of pine in this instance is most effective, lending a sense of peasant character to the piece. The open display area is compelling in its intensity. Hanging cabinets are finding more and more favor in the modern home. Their effectiveness is unquestioned. They tend to break the bleakness of the barren wall. This is a colorful model that would fit gracefully into a modern interior.

BREWSTER ARMCHAIR

Metropolitan Museum of Art   Gift of Mrs. J. Insley Blair, 1951

Very few Brewster armchairs of this quality are now in existence. The fault is certainly not in their sound construction. In the 17th century chairs were scarce in the households. They were only reserved for the use of the master of the house. This model is dated *circa* 1650 and is from Massachusetts. It is made of hickory and ash. It is in the collection of the American Wing of the Metropolitan Museum of Art. The manifold turn-ings are varied and decisive. The finials on the top of the back posts are delightful. There probably is a rush seat which is hidden by the loose cushion. These chairs were named after an official of the *S.S. Mayflower*. It is believed that several of these chairs were actually brought over from England in the vessel. However, this has never been veri-fied. This model is certainly massive and is en-cased in a forest of turnings.

HIGH CHEST ON A STAND
Philadelphia Museum of Art

This William and Mary high chest is made of curly maple on pine. It has herringbone borders surrounding the drawers. It is Pennsylvania German of the 18th century. There are two small drawers near the top and three drawers below of varying sizes. In the stand there are three drawers as shown. The apron is broken by a series of compass curves and supported by six trumpet-turned legs. There is a flat shaped stretcher which holds them together. All this is supported by six bun feet. These chests were built at this time to hold so many of the little articles that plague every housekeeper. This piece is especially attractive by reason of the matched curly maple veneers on the drawer fronts and elsewhere. The drop pulls are of the period but the cut-out escutcheon plates are a bit unusual. All in all, this is a most attractive and useful high chest of drawers. It is in the collection of the Philadelphia Museum of Art.

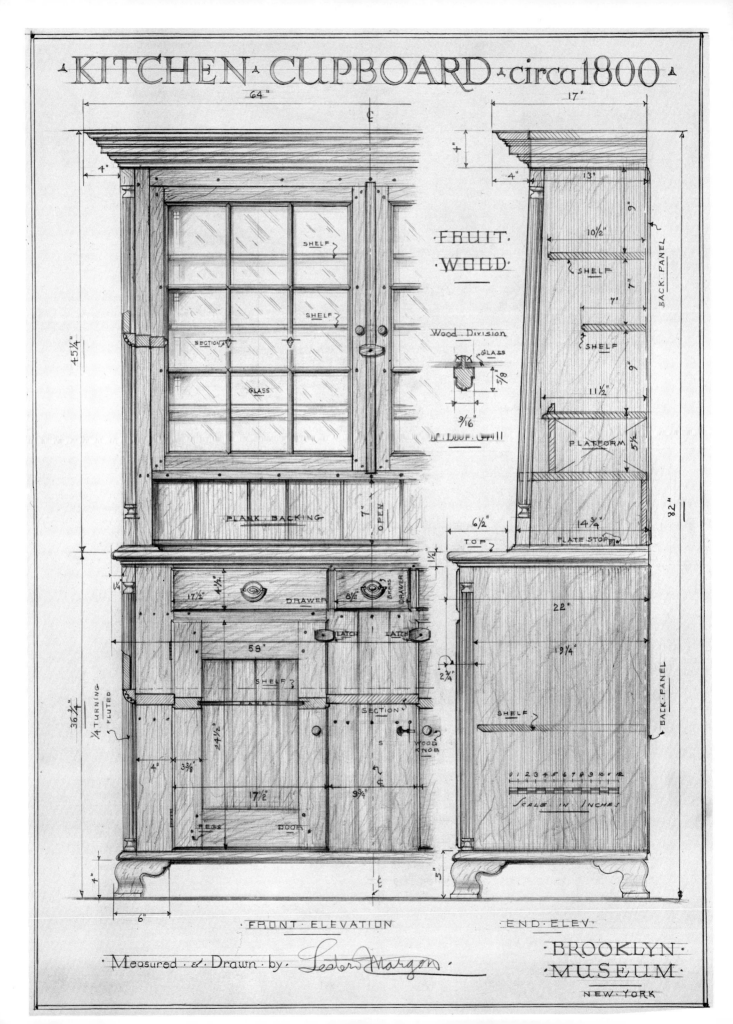

KITCHEN CUPBOARD circa 1800

FRUIT WOOD

Wood Division

64"

17"

4"

45¾"

SHELF

SHELF

SECTION

GLASS

GLASS

9/16"

5/8"

OF DOOR

13"

9"

10½"

SHELF

7"

7"

SHELF

9"

11½"

PLATFORM

5½"

BACK PANEL

82"

PLANK BACKING

7"

OPEN

1½"

6½"

TOP

14¾"

PLATE STOP

22"

19¼"

¼"

17½"

4½"

DRAWER

8½"

BRASS

DRAWER

LATCH

LATCH

58"

SHELF

PANEL

SECTION

WOOD KNOB

2¾"

BACK PANEL

SHELF

36¾"

¼ TURNING

FLUTED

4"

3⅜"

24½"

17½"

9¾"

PEGS

DOOR

7"

6"

5"

0 1 2 3 4 5 6 7 8 9 10 11 12

SCALE IN INCHES

FRONT ELEVATION

END ELEV

BROOKLYN MUSEUM

NEW YORK

Measured & Drawn by Lester Morgan

KITCHEN CABINET

Brooklyn Museum   The Monroe and Estelle Hewlett Collection

Kitchen cupboards were very useful adjuncts in Colonial farmhouses. This model, made from soft fruit wood, closely grained, dates from *circa* 1800, probably from Pennsylvania. Its wide usefulness is evidenced by the two-door lower cabinet for storage. Above are three drawers for cooking utensils. There is an open shelf work area. Above is a large two-door glass-enclosed cabinet for the display of glassware and china. This piece is rather late for this type of kitchen cabinet. It shows a mixture of provincialism and classicism. The heavy protruding cornice, the use of quarter round columns on the corners and the nicely shaped bracket legs with planks for panels and backings is a

strange combination. The piece is interesting if a bit controversial. The cupboard is placed in the Estelle Hewlett Court in the museum. The interior of the upper display cabinet is painted green and antiqued. The wood is finished in a soft molasses tan and very effective. The shelves are grooved to set plates vertically and there is a projection for the display of spoons. The cupboard is certainly utilitarian and would find favor in any kitchen. At an earlier date these kitchen cabinets were made in New York by the Dutch. These cabinets were of goodly proportions and often profusely painted and decorated.

KITCHEN CUPBOARD
Old Sturbridge Village

The Village Furniture Collection at Old Sturbridge Village in Massachusetts is so varied because it departs from the traditional forms. Many pieces of this country furniture were made by the town's joiners which may account for the strange individuality of some of the pieces. This 17th century kitchen cupboard of chestnut has a cupboard below for the keeping of the kitchen's pots and pans. The open shelves above are particularly suited for the display of pewter of that period.

This piece resembles a cabinet in the Du Pont bequest in the House of the Miller of Millbach in the Philadelphia Museum of Art. These cupboards are distinctly impressive by reason of their height and peasant character. Note the plank backing of the open shelving. The extended cornice may permit indirect lighting in the present day interior. These old pieces are sought after by collectors but are difficult to find.

PAINTED AND DECORATED CHEST OF DRAWERS

The Henry Francis du Pont Winterthur Museum

This chest of drawers from Ipswich, Massachusetts, *circa* 1678, is made of oak and other woods. It is painted as well as carved and decorated. There are applied half-turnings, carved mouldings, painted and decorated panels and sunken panels surrounded by mouldings. There is also strap-work on two of the lower drawers. This is the type of strap-work that may be found on many Massachusetts cupboards of the period. This chest of drawers is so interesting because it shows the tendency towards over-decoration at this time. Note that the legs are continuations of the corner posts. The turned wooden knobs are accentuated by painted designs as the background. This dated Stanford family chest of drawers is in the collection of the Henry Francis du Pont Winterthur Museum.

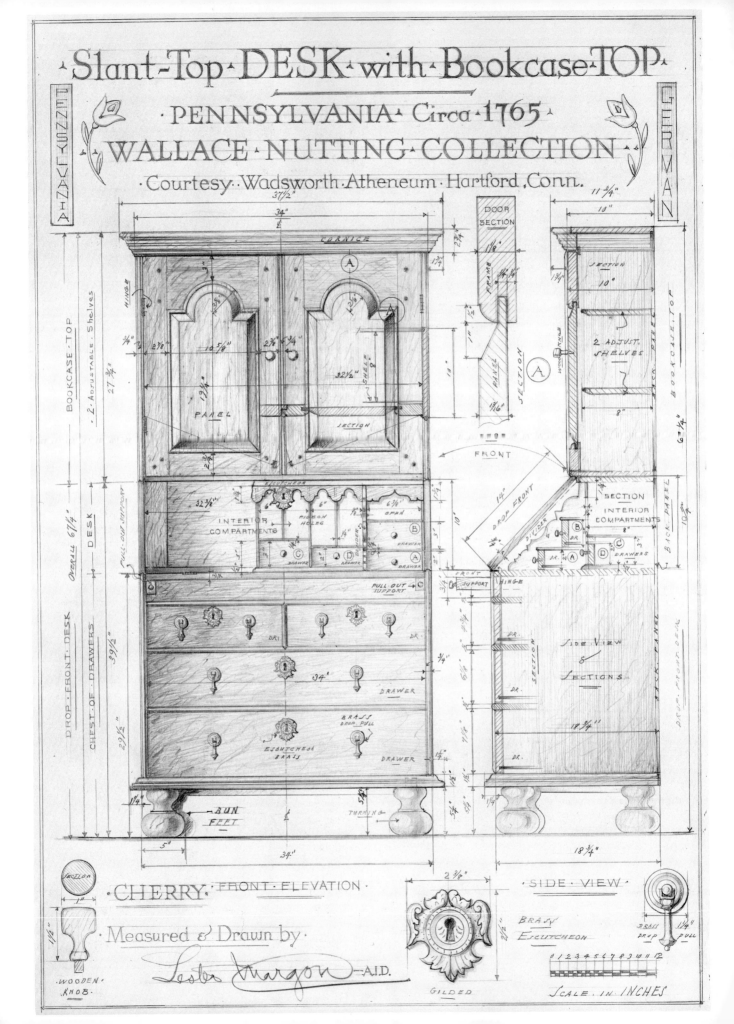

Slant-Top DESK with Bookcase TOP

PENNSYLVANIA Circa 1765
WALLACE NUTTING COLLECTION
Courtesy Wadsworth Atheneum Hartford, Conn.

PENNSYLVANIA

GERMAN

CHERRY · FRONT · ELEVATION ·

· Measured & Drawn by ·

Lester Margon - A.I.D.

WOODEN KNOB

BRASS ESCUTCHEON

GILDED

· SIDE · VIEW ·

0 1 2 3 4 5 6 7 8 9 10 11 12

SCALE IN INCHES

SLANT-TOP DESK WITH BOOKCASE TOP

Wadsworth Atheneum, Hartford   Wallace Nutting Collection

The popular designation of furniture and crafts called "Pennsylvania Dutch" is not correct. These settlers came from the Rhine Valley under the sponsorship of William Penn. Therefore the correct name should be "Pennsylvania German." They were of a sturdy stock and worked diligently. Settling originally in the vicinity of Philadelphia they soon spread into Easton, Baltimore and Pittsburgh. They brought with them fond memories of the *Vaterland* and an innate appreciation of the decorative arts. As soon as their barest needs were accomplished, they turned their attention to better housing and finer furniture. This tall piece is in the Wallace Nutting Collection of the Wadsworth Atheneum. In reality it is a composite chest of drawers and drop-front desk with a separate bookcase top. Cherry was the favored wood because it was found in abundance in the vicinity of Philadelphia. There could have been no better choice, for cherry wood has a velvety softness and ages with a patina that is truly beneficent. Naturally, most of the furniture was inspired by memories of European pieces but because of the lack of tools their cabinetmaking had to be simplified. This gives Pennsylvania German furniture a vitality and sturdiness that is its mark of distinction. This combination piece is certainly sophisticated but its simplicity remains. It is this informality that makes it so irresistable.

79

DESK AND BOOKCASE

Colonial Williamsburg, Williamsburg, Virginia

In this desk and bookcase, the primary wood is cherry, the secondary wood Southern Yellow Pine. Made *circa* 1780-1800, it was found in Alexandria, Virginia. It is now part of the furnishings in the Raleigh Tavern Parlor in Williamsburg. It is a piece of monumental proportions with revealing details. The scroll top with the turned finials produces the necessary lightness and the breaking of the door panelling reduces the otherwise great height. The bracket feet, the applied quarter columns at the corners, the bead around the drawers, all these details makes the piece acceptable. In the Raleigh Tavern most of the furniture is American-made, which adds to the comeliness of the surroundings. This is a most useful piece combining a bookcase top with a desk compartment and a chest of drawers below.

DESK-BOOKCASE

Heritage Foundation, Deerfield

One of the rarest pieces of furniture in the Deerfield Museum of the Heritage Foundation is this mahogany Chippendale kettle-base secretary. It is of Boston origin and graces the Dwight-Barnard House, Old Deerfield, Massachusetts. Despite its varied plans and great height, this combination piece of chest of drawers, drop-front desk and bookcase top, is imposing. The pulls and the escutcheon plates are amazing. The separate bookcase top is distinguished by the reeded pilasters at the sides and the shaped panelled doors. Above is a Classical cornice with a broken pediment, with a flamelike urn turning at the center. It is a piece that is so distinctively individual that a duplicate may never have been made. That is the excitement of American furniture. It is full of surprises.

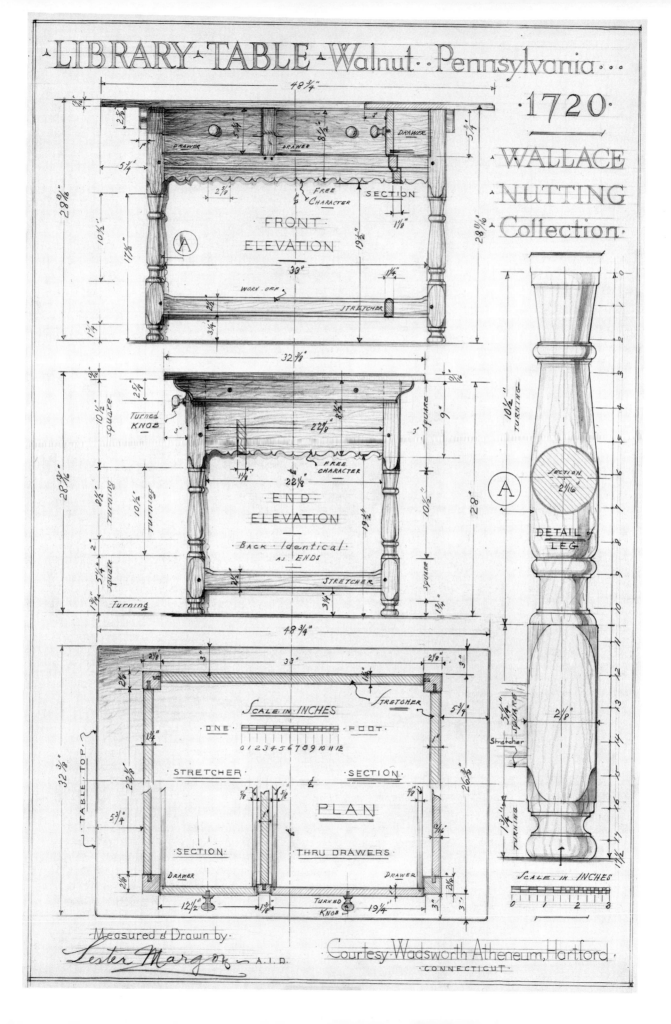

LIBRARY TABLE Walnut · Pennsylvania

1720

WALLACE NUTTING Collection

FRONT ELEVATION

END ELEVATION

Back · Identical as ENDS

FREE CHARACTER

SECTION

STRETCHER

WORN OFF

DRAWER

Turned KNOB

DETAIL of LEG

SECTION 2 1/16

TURNING

SQUARE

PLAN

STRETCHER   SECTION

SECTION   THRU DRAWERS

TABLE TOP

DRAWER   Turned KNOB   DRAWER

SCALE IN INCHES
ONE FOOT
0 1 2 3 4 5 6 7 8 9 10 11 12

SCALE IN INCHES
0 1 2 3

· Measured & Drawn by ·
Lester Margon — A.I.D.

LIBRARY TABLE

Wadsworth Atheneum, Hartford   *Wallace Nutting Collection*

This walnut library table from Pennsylvania dates from *circa* 1720. It has an extended top held in place by the addition of two side brackets. There are two drawers, oddly enough, of different sizes. The leg turnings are provincial in character. The shaped apron is engaging in its repeat scroll design. The four legs are held in place by straight stretchers. So much for the technical data concerning this table. Library tables were much favored in Colonial homes. Often set against the back of a settee, they formed a handsome grouping. Coming from Pennsylvania, this table is in keeping with the type of furniture made by these Pennsylvania German settlers. The table is unpretentious and honest in its design and workmanship. The walnut is straight-grained with only a meagre amount of finish, to permit the lustre of the walnut to shine through. Part of the Wallace Nutting Collection at the Wadsworth Atheneum, it again shows the excellent taste of this collector. The turnings have a special crude majesty. They are different and distinctive. The back is identical with the front with the exception that the drawers are omitted. In this instance the brackets at the sides give the table a rustic eloquence.

SLANT-TOP DESK

The Wadsworth Atheneum, Hartford   The Wallace Nutting Collection

One of the most original and typical pieces created by the Early American cabinetmakers is the slant-top desk on a stand. This excellent model is in the fabulous Wallace Nutting Collection of the Wadsworth Atheneum in Hartford, Connecticut. The collection was presented to the museum by Mr. J. Pierpont Morgan. It is a large assemblage with many room settings. This desk is made of fruitwood with the date *circa* 1700. The refinement of the leg turnings indicates that it may have been made in Massachusetts. The top is hinged. When lifted up, a few small drawers and a series of pigeon-holes are revealed. There is a large area for storage. The four legs are held in place by a shaped crossed stretcher. Note how the ends are plainly dovetailed into the front. A bead surrounds the lower drawer. One thing about these Early American pieces is that they are honest. There is no attempt to camouflage anything. The top is plainly hinged with a wrought iron butterfly design. Below the top is an unadorned keyhole but on the drawer below are two drop pulls. This desk is particularly interesting because it fulfills its purpose without undo pretense.

PENNSYLVANIA GERMAN TABLE

Philadelphia Museum of Art

This Moravian table in walnut, *circa* 1730-1750, is a good example of Pennsylvania German craftsmanship. The stark turned legs are connected by outside stretchers held together by pegs. There are two drawers of different sizes and a scalloped apron featuring the endeared heart motif at the center. There is a plank top with wide overhangs at the sides. The construction is massive and resembles tables of the Jacobean period. These Pennsylvania German people were simple folk and their furniture reflects the primitive arts of the homeland. Much of the furniture was painted and decorated with floral and religious subjects. The principal centers were Allentown, Reading, Bethlehem, Lancaster and York. The Pennsylvania German mode of living has not radically changed throughout the years. Emigrating from the Rhine Valley in 1683 to escape religious persecution, under the sponsorship of William Penn, they have contributed much to the folk art of America.

· FOLDING · CARD · TABLE ·

· MUSEUM · OF · THE · CITY · OF · NEW · YORK ·

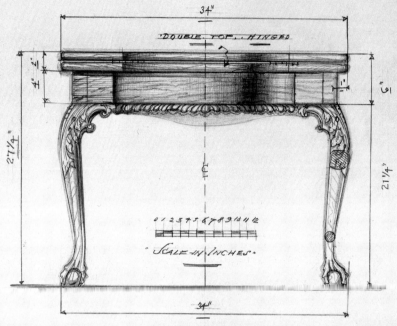

· DOUBLE · TOP · HINGED ·

34"

27½"

21¼"

0 1 2 3 4 5 6 7 8 9 10 11 12
· SCALE · IN · INCHES ·

34"

· FRONT · VIEW ·

· MAHOGANY ·

· Circa ·
1760 - 1780 ·

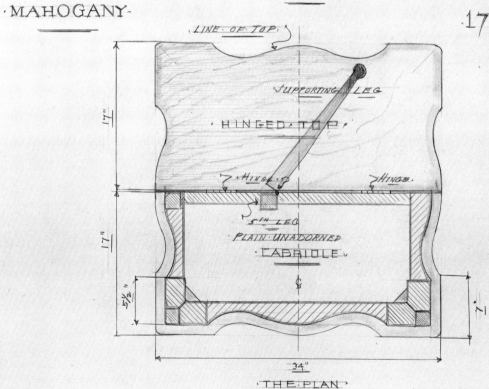

· LINE · OF · TOP ·

· SUPPORTING · LEG ·

· HINGED · TOP ·

17"

· HINGE ·   · HINGE ·

5TH LEG
· PLAIN · UNADORNED ·
· CABRIOLE ·

17"

5½"

7"

34"

· THE · PLAN ·

Measured & Drawn by Lester Margon

FOLDING CARD TABLE

The Museum of the City of New York
From the Collection of Mrs. J. Insley Blair, mother of the donor, Mrs. Screven Lorillard

This Chippendale card table with a double top was made of mahogany *circa* 1760-1780. It is from New York. In the Colonial living rooms a card table was an accepted part of the furnishings. Especially convenient were the card tables with double tops that could be closed when not in use and set aside. The most distinguished part of this one is the ultra-refined cabriole legs with the acanthus carving at the knee which tapers off into the ball-and-claw feet. The gadroon carving below the apron is most effective. The shaped plan is full of wonder and excitement and is found only on the very best tables of the period. Note that

there is a fifth leg to support the top when opened. This leg can be of the simplest cabriole design. In its simplicity there is elegance and in its candor are depths of feeling. The richness of the straight-grained mahogany is compelling. This designer appreciated the truism that it is not necessary to incorporate fireworks in a design to make it worthy. There is eloquence in simplicity and cognizance in restraint. This is a table that one could live with in peace and tranquility. It is in the collection of Mrs. J. Insley Blair of the Museum of the City of New York.

87

LOOKING-GLASS

The Henry Francis du Pont Winterthur Museum

This mahogany and gilt looking-glass was made in Philadelphia by James and Henry Reynolds, *circa* 1790. A label on the backboard noted its authenticity. Although this frame was made in the Federal period, the Chippendale details were retained. The gilded carved phoenix and the indented corners of the frame are in reality more typical of the preceding Georgian period. The mirror is quite large, measuring 49¼″ x 24½″. Of special interest is the design of the fretwork at the top and bottom. Its rhythm is magnificent and the circular cutout at the top brings the phoenix into proper prominence. These mirrors were generally hung above the mantlepiece and reflected the elegance of the living rooms. This looking glass is in the collection of the Henry Francis du Pont Winterthur Museum.

DRESSING TABLE

Heritage Foundation, Deerfield

The museum of the Heritage Foundation at Deerfield, Massachusetts, has probably the finest collection of Connecticut Valley furniture in existence. This dressing table is in walnut veneers, from *circa* 1726-1730. It is in the Queen Anne style. The lower center drawer is decorated with a carved and gilded shell motif, and the two acorn-shaped pendants are also gilded. This dressing table is in the Sheldon-Hawks House at Old Deerfield.

The brass pulls and escutcheon plates are imposing. There are two upper drawers and three drawers below. The carved Spanish feet are of an earlier date. Deerfield is a charming Colonial village in the Connecticut Valley. The houses contain examples of American furniture from simple country origin to the finest products of the famed cabinetmakers.

LIST OF ILLUSTRATIONS

(Asterisks indicate photographs accompanied by measured drawings.)

SURVEY OF AMERICAN FURNITURE PERIODS

Very few examples of furniture made in America prior to 1650 have survived. These early pieces were based on English Jacobean models, 1603-1649. This furniture was massive with the use of oak predominating, although various other woods were incorporated, including pine, ash and poplar. Many of the chests of drawers were carved, with the use of applied split turnings, bulbous posts and legs with bun feet. In many instances, sunken panels were painted and decorated with geometric tracery in white, red and green. The few chairs that we know of were of the "stick" variety. They were known as Brewster and Carver, named after two officials of the Massachusetts Bay Colony. These chairs had turned posts with many spindles. The back posts were often crowned with bobbin turnings. It is believed that several of these chairs were actually brought over on the Mayflower. Simple wainscot chairs were introduced, fashioned after the wainscoting that adorned the walls of many of the better homes. The twisted turning became popular for tables and was also used for stretchers. When upholstery was used it was either a crude homespun material or leather. Turkey work was also popular.

EARLY AMERICAN FURNITURE, 1650-1700

Many examples of the furniture of this period may be seen in the great museum collections in the American Wing of the Metropolitan Museum of Art in New York City and at the Henry Francis du Pont Winterthur Museum near Wilmington, Delaware. These collections prove that the styles of the Mother Country were copied more or less faithfully. Certain new types of furniture were introduced over here such as the "butterfly" table, Hadley chests and court cupboards. In many instances American innovations may be noted. These included the alleviation of undo carving and ornamentation, with special emphasis being put on line, form and proportions. Stools and benches were used, with the application of loose cushions. Chests were made extensively and were put on higher legs which produced court, press and livery cupboards and finally what is known as the highboy. Many of the court cupboards were used for the storage of food. In these instances the upper doors had pierced carving for ventilation. These cupboards were generally constructed in two pieces. Oak continued to be the favored wood. These cupboards became the decorative objects of a room. The chairs were heavy with much carving, and featured applied half turnings. Often in the backs of the chairs appeared portrait medallions.

THE WILLIAM AND MARY INFLUENCE, 1700-1725

The dawn of the 18th century saw the increase in the American economy. Fine houses were being built and suitably furnished. The woods favored were walnut, maple and veneered pine. Tall chests of drawers with desk compartments with fronts that dropped down were show-pieces of the times. Lowboys and highboys with trumpet turned legs and shaped crossed stretchers were favored. In New York, massive kitchen cabinets were made, often decorated with "grisaille" paintings in gray monotone. Oval gate-leg dining tables with drop leaves were supported by clusters of turned legs on swivel mechanisms. The period introduced Japanese and Chinese lacquer work in floral and scenic decorations. Known as the Age of Walnut, with the introduction of marquetry this embellishment was featured in floral designs with the combination of colored woods. The seaweed variety of marquetry consisted of rambling forms of minute tracery. For upholstery, velvets, damasks, crewel embroidery and needlepoint were used. It was a period of change and elaboration in all forms of furniture. As is usually the case, with prosperity comes extravagance. The affluent rivalled one another as to who could have the most elegant furniture and trappings. Wall panelling was favored and the mantlepiece became the focal point of many living rooms, with portraits featured.

THE QUEEN ANNE STYLE, 1725-1760

The principal innovation of the Queen Anne style, as interpreted in America, was the preference for the curvilinear line. The almost universal use of the cabriole leg on chairs, lowboys and highboys was enhanced by the addition of the varied shaping of the skirtings, characterized by acorn appendages. This produced a merry sense of movement which became very evident in combination with the "bonnet" tops on the highboys. Carving was featured, with the use of the ball and claw foot. Tea tables found favor and a card table became a feature in most living rooms. Chairs were used without stretchers, featuring carved cabriole legs. On seating pieces, upholstered slip seats were used. Many pieces were completely upholstered in fine fabrics. Tilt-top tables, with pie-crust borders on the top, became a necessity, for space-saving reasons, in the living rooms. Tall cabinets, encased in glass, were featured for display, with the ever increasing vogue for collecting. The introduction of a variety of cabinet woods was inevitable. In interiors the rooms became larger and the ceilings higher, with wall panelling, featuring columns, pilasters and architectural investiture. Cornices and entabletures were often too massive for the size of the rooms. It was a period when elaboration became the order of the times without the needed sense of restraint.

THE CHIPPENDALE PENETRATION IN AMERICA, 1750-1790

With the publication of the "Gentleman and Cabinetmaker's Directory" in 1754, Thomas Chippendale's fame as the foremost furniture designer and cabinetmaker became evident. His fame soon influenced furniture making throughout Europe and America. The intricacies evident in this style included favor of the serpentine front plan, the predominance of carving and the introduction of the block front. Chinese fret-work and Japanese lacquer were featured. Architectural details were incorporated in the designs and the use of the quarter columnette on the front corners of case-goods became a must. The bracket foot was used on pieces approaching the floor. Mirrors of Rococo design, carved, painted and gilded, found favor. This period took inspiration from many sources and had little regard for its derivation. French, Chinese, Irish and Mediterranean influences were used indiscriminately. It was a period that knew no bounds but was most prolific in adaptation if not invention. One of the features of this period in America was the making of the fabulous Philadelphia highboys. Tall clocks were popular especially in halls, and the design of chairs surpassed the imagination. Especially elaborate were the Chippendale chairs featuring fanciful pierced center back splats and ribband fantasies. Many of these chairs were beyond comprehension and showed Chippendale's mastery in this particular field.

THE FEDERAL PERIOD, 1785-1840

Robert Adam in England inaugurated a new style in furniture design and the treatment of interiors. Influenced by the excavations being carried on in Pompeii and Herculaneum, he used Classical motifs almost exclusively. It was not until 1790 that the trend became evident in America. Due to the establishment of the Federal Government in Washington, this style became known as "Federal." The use of paint replaced wood panelling and satinwood was favored for furniture, although mahogany still was used. A preponderance of applied plaster decoration of the Neoclassic type appeared on walls and ceilings. For the first time a definite effort was made to achieve a unity in form, ornament and furniture in an interior. This effort was enhanced by the use of architectural details for the background. While Adam was not a cabinetmaker, he did supervise all the work undertaken. In America this style found its way into the design of many articles of household use. This was followed by the Empire style in France, glorifying the victories of Napoleon on the battlefield. Napoleon enlisted the services of the architects Perçier and Fontaine, who created a style that expressed the military trend. Eagles, stars, shields, banners, lances and thunder-bolts were some of the symbols used in this furniture and decoration. The tendency spread to America, but was never really successful.

A Brief Bibliography

Since "More American Furniture Treasures" is not a history of American furniture, a brief bibliography has been included. Further study of the subject will be advanced by reference to these particular books.

The Encyclopedia of American Furniture, J. Aronson
English and American Furniture, H. Cescinsky
Furniture Masterpieces of Duncan Phyfe, C. O. Cornelius
Colonial Interiors, L. French, Jr.
Furniture of Our Forefathers, E. Singleton
18th Century American Arts, E. J. Hipkiss
Colonial Furniture in America, L. V. Lockwood
Furniture Treasury, W. Nutting
The Standard Book of American Antiques, E. G. Miller, Jr.
Fine Points of Early American Furniture, A. Sack
Elements of Interior Decoration, S. Whiton

DOUGH·BOX·&·KNEADING·TRAY

PHILADELPHIA·MUSEUM·OF·ART·

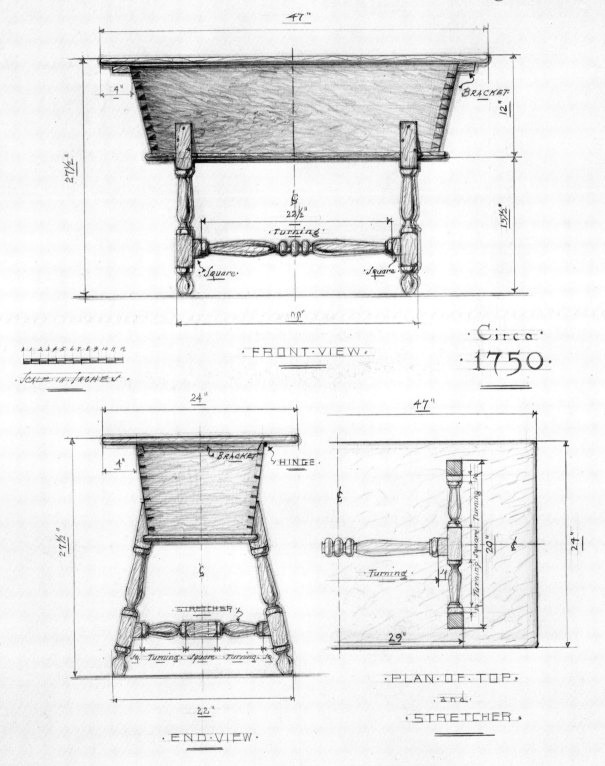

47"

4"

BRACKET

12"

27½"

15½"

₵

22½"

Turning

·Square·   ·Square·

22"

·FRONT·VIEW·

·Circa·
·1750·

·SCALE·IN·INCHES·

24"

1"

BRACKET   HINGE

27½"

₵

STRETCHER

Sq. Turning Square Turning Sq.

22"

·END·VIEW·

47"

₵

Turning Square Turning

20"

24"

·Turning·

29"

·PLAN·OF·TOP·
·and·
·STRETCHER·

·Measured·&·Drawn·by· Lester Margon·

DOUGH BOX AND KNEADING TRAY
Philadelphia Museum of Art

In recent years antiques from the counties of the
Pennsylvania German settlers have been receiving
more and more attention. These unique people,
their old world customs and their colorful folk
art are today a source of inspiration. Their furniture was simple, utilitarian and peasant in character. In contrast to the more elegant styles of the
period this furniture was staunch and credible. In
the Philadelphia Museum of Art there are several
rooms from the House of the Miller of Millbach,

a gift of the Du Ponts, that affords a splendid setting for this Pennsylvania German furniture. This
dough box with kneading tray is one of these
pieces. The wife prepared a good quantity of
dough and placed it in the box for storage. When
needed, a portion of the dough was placed on the
tray and kneaded. This piece shows the ingenious
method of construction in the way the box is held
as in a cradle of the sturdy turned base below.

CARVER TYPE SIDE CHAIR

Metropolitan Museum of Art   Gift of Mrs. Russell Sage, 1909

Coming from New England, this Carver type side chair is dated *circa* 1650-1700. It is a model said to have been brought over in the *S.S. Mayflower*. Its simplicity is disarming with the rush seat held firmly between the front legs and the rear posts. The finials on the back posts are interesting. The legs are held in place by plain stretchers. Made principally of oak, other woods were incorporated in these chairs. These are the first chairs that were brought into this country and show no particular period influences. They were sturdy and attractive in their simplicity. This model is in the American Wing of the Metropolitan Museum of Art.

98

CARVER TYPE ARMCHAIR

Metropolitan Museum of Art   Gift of Mrs. Russell Sage, 1909

A bit more attractive, this Carver type armchair dates from the Pilgrim Century, *circa* 1650-1700. These chairs were named after an officer of the *S.S. Mayflower*. Note that the rush seat is set in between the front legs and the rear posts, both of which are turned and have finials. The back is composed of horizontal turnings intercepted by three vertical turnings. These early chairs give the impression of the honesty and straightforwardness of the Pilgrim Fathers. There is little pretense, just an effort to produce a chair that will be serviceable. Despite its evident simplicity there is a certain grandeur about this armchair that speaks well for its maker. The chair is in the American Wing of the Metropolitan Museum of Art.

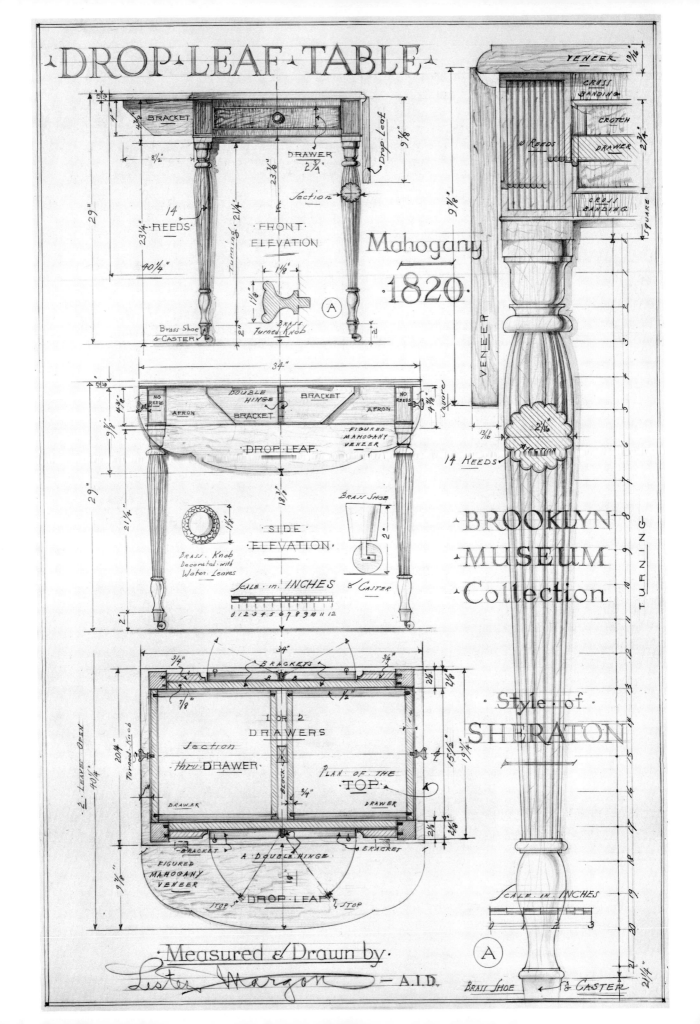

DROP·LEAF·TABLE

Mahogany
1820

BROOKLYN
MUSEUM
Collection

Style · of ·
SHERATON

Front Elevation

BRACKET
DRAWER 2¾"
Section
FRONT ELEVATION
14 REEDS
29"
23¾"
Turning 2¼"
8½"
9⅞"
40¼"
A
Brass Shoe & Caster
Brass Turned Knob
1⅛"
1⅛"
2"
2"
2"
Drop Leaf

Side Elevation

34"
DOUBLE HINGE
BRACKET
APRON
BRACKET
APRON
NO REEDS
NO REEDS
DROP·LEAF
FIGURED MAHOGANY VENEER
SIDE ELEVATION
29"
21¼"
9⅛"
4¾"
18½"
Brass Knob Decorated with Water Leaves
1⅛"
21"
BRASS SHOE & CASTER
2"
Scale in INCHES
0 1 2 3 4 5 6 7 8 9 10 11 12

Plan of the Top / Section thru Drawer

34"
BRACKETS
¾"
¾"
1⅛"
½"
2⅜"
2⅛"
1 OR 2 DRAWERS
Section thru DRAWER
BLOCK
¾"
PLAN OF THE TOP
DRAWER
DRAWER
15½"
19¾"
2 Leaves Open 40¼"
20¼"
Turned Knob
9⅛"
2⅜"
2⅛"
BRACKET
A DOUBLE HINGE
BRACKET
FIGURED MAHOGANY VENEER
STOP
DROP·LEAF
STOP

Leg detail (right)

VENEER
CROSS BANDING
CROTCH
DRAWER
10 REEDS
CROSS BANDING
VENEER
1⁹⁄₁₆
2¾"
SQUARE
14 REEDS
2⁵⁄₁₆
SECTION
13⁄₁₆
TURNING
1
2
3
4
5
6
7
8
9
10
11
12
13
14
15
16
17
18
19
20
21
2¼"
Scale in INCHES
0 1 2 3
A
BRASS SHOE & CASTER

Measured & Drawn by
Lester Margon — A.I.D.

DROP-LEAF TABLE
Brooklyn Museum

The Brooklyn Museum houses a series of American rooms completely furnished in the various periods. There is a living room from the Sewell House from Maryland, 1665, a dining room from the Corbin House from North Carolina, 1758, and the exterior and ground floor interior from the Schenck House from Canarsie, Long Island, 1775, and several others. This elegant drop-leaf table in the Sheraton style is made of mahogany and dated 1820. It might be considered to be in the style of the School of Duncan Phyfe. Some of the features of this table are the elegantly turned and reeded legs and the drawer with the raised bead around the perimeter. The mahogany is selected, rich,

and finely figured. The drawer knob is jewel-like in perfection. The furniture attributed to Thomas Sheraton is distinguished by grace of line, lightness of structure and elegance of proportions. This type of furniture fits well into the small house and today's apartments. With the two drop leaves, it is space-saving and adequate for limited dining. In this model the legs are the pièce de résistance and warrant study and attention. The finesse of the turned members and euphony of the contour are outstanding. The furniture of Thomas Sheraton evokes the stately grandeur of Colonial Salem. It is furniture for the élite.

LAMP TABLE

Wadsworth Atheneum, Hartford   The Wallace Nutting Collection

In Colonial homes, lamp tables were very popular. They were of many sizes and shapes. This octagonal top lamp table from Plymouth, Massachusetts, dates from *circa* 1690-1700. The woods used are maple and pine. The design influence is Queen Anne. Again, it is from the Wallace Nutting Collection of the Wadsworth Atheneum in Hartford, Connecticut. At first glance the table appears to be rather simple, but on closer investigation that is not the case. It is quite large and the overhanging top casts deep shadows. The turnings are well delineated and are held in place by a straight stretcher. The shaped apron, on four sides, is in-terestingly cut to give a certain oriental appearance. We have become accustomed to so much elaboration in furniture design that when we come across a rather unpretentious piece we are nonplussed. We forget that there can be elegance in simplicity and grandeur in the unadorned. This lamp table was included with the purpose of showing a contrast with other pieces that are more complicated and ostentatious. It is a table for many uses. With its adequate size and height it lends itself not alone to hold a lamp but affords space for many other accessories that are needed in the living room.

GATE-LEG TABLE

The Brooklyn Museum   Gift of Luke Vincent Lockwood

This elegant gate-leg table, with walnut top and fruitwood base, was possibly made in Pennsylvania, *circa* 1710. Here is a strictly American conception. In no other period or country do we find a multitudinous gate-leg table with drop leaves that opens into an oval top dining table of goodly proportions. When closed, the table can serve as a useful side table or console. Aside from its prodigious utilitarian aspect, the table should be recognized for the beauty of the turnings and the carved Spanish feet. The turning process is an art. It requires not only skill but a fine sense of line and proportion. It is a very exacting process to put a square block of wood on a lathe, and by the magic of pressing a blade against the revolving wood, create the intricacies of the turning. This table is in the American Rooms of the Brooklyn Museum. It is the gift of Luke Vincent Lockwood.

TILT-TOP · TABLE · Mahogany · 1800

·METROPOLITAN · MUSEUM · OF · ART · N.Y.

· Gift of Mrs. RUSSELL · SAGE ·

· 1909 ·

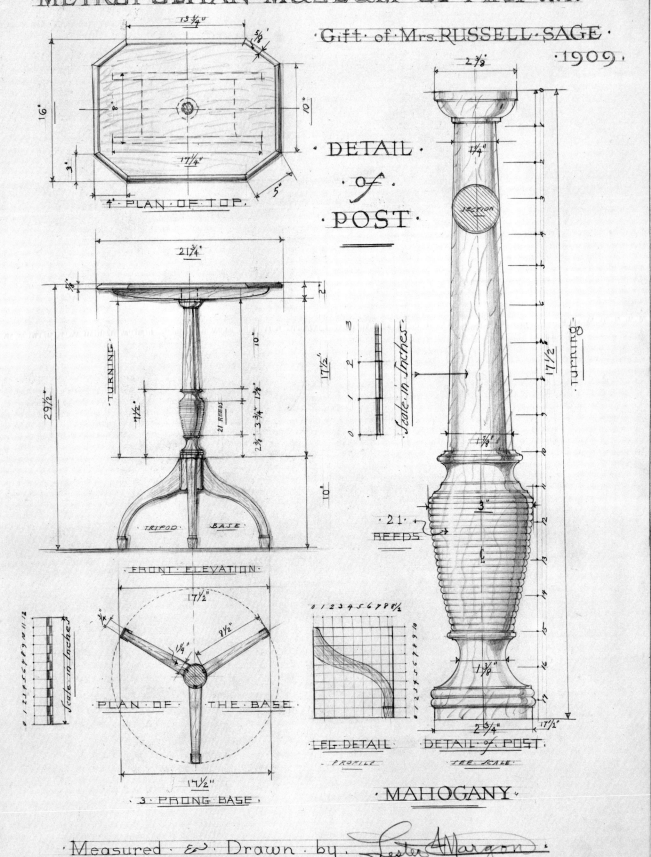

· PLAN · OF · TOP ·

· DETAIL · of · POST ·

· Scale · in · Inches ·

· TURNING ·

· 21 REEDS ·

· TRIPOD · BASE ·

· FRONT · ELEVATION ·

· Scale · in · Inches ·

· PLAN · OF · THE · BASE ·

· 3 · PRONG · BASE ·

· LEG · DETAIL ·

· PROFILE ·

· 21 REEDS ·

· SECTION ·

· Turning ·

· DETAIL · of · POST ·

· SEE · SCALE ·

· MAHOGANY ·

· Measured · & · Drawn · by · Lester A. Margon ·

AMERICAN TILT-TOP TABLE

Metropolitan Museum of Art   Gift of Mrs. Russell Sage, 1909

This Sheraton style tilt-top table, *circa* 1800, in mahogany, is a splendid example of the meticulous cabinet-work that was produced at this time. Its Federal implications are evident. The excellent standard is eloquent by reason of the unusual multitudinous horizontal reedings in the lower section. It is a small table with an octagonal tray-like top. This type of tilt-top table was very popular at this time in the living rooms. After tea was served, the table could be readily removed or set aside. The tripod base is decisive in its simple delineation and typical of the Sheraton influence.

The beauty of this table has all the delicacy of a piece of jewelry. It is the work of a master who has given it all his study and loving care. Pieces like this are rare. It is another splendid gift of Mrs. Russell Sage to the American Wing. Her good taste and judgment are evident in the selection of these pieces of furniture with which her name is connected. The mechanism of the tilt-top is simple. There are several recognized methods, all of which are applicable. The finish is adequate, but not heavy, so that the beauty of the wood can show through.

ARMCHAIR, SCHOOL OF DUNCAN PHYFE

Cooper-Hewitt Museum of Design   Smithsonian Institution

This mahogany armchair, a companion piece to the side chair, New York, 1812, was probably made by Duncan Phyfe. It is also in the collection of the Cooper-Hewitt Museum of Design in New York. While the chair has many features that are associated with the work of the master cabinet-maker there are reasons to doubt its authenticity. The way the arm curves and fits into the turned support is not typical. The legs are too Louis XVI. The turnings are not just right. However, both the side, and the armchair are engaging pieces. After a student has studied many examples of the work of Duncan Phyfe he can instinctively know if a piece is an original. This chair should be designated "from the School of Duncan Phyfe."

SIDE CHAIR, SCHOOL OF DUNCAN PHYFE

Cooper-Hewitt Museum of Design   Smithsonian Institution

This mahogany side chair was probably made by Duncan Phyfe, New York, *circa* 1812. It is in the collection of the Cooper-Hewitt Museum of Design which is now associated with the Smithsonian Institution of Washington. While there is no definite proof that it was actually made by the master cabinetmaker, the chair contains salient characteristics of his work. They are the heavily reeded seat frame and the cross pieces of the back. The top panel of the back is carved in the familiar tied dart design. The only parts of the side chair that may be questionable are the use of cane for the seat and the front legs which resemble the Louis XVI style. However, it is an engaging chair that affords the opportunity for comparison.

· TAVERN · TABLE ·
· BROOKLYN · MUSEUM ·
NEW · YORK ·

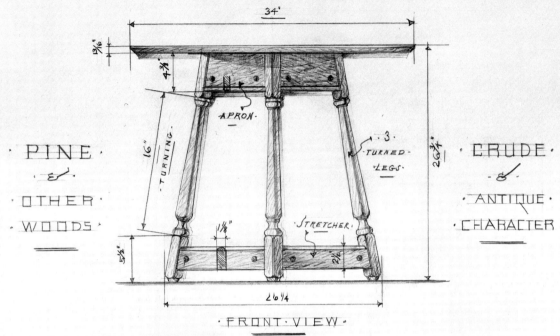

· PINE ·
&
· OTHER ·
· WOODS ·

· CRUDE ·
&
· ANTIQUE ·
· CHARACTER ·

34"

9/16"

4¾"

APRON

16" TURNING

· 3 ·
TURNED
LEGS

26¾"

1⅛"

STRETCHER

5½"

2½"

26¼

· FRONT · VIEW ·

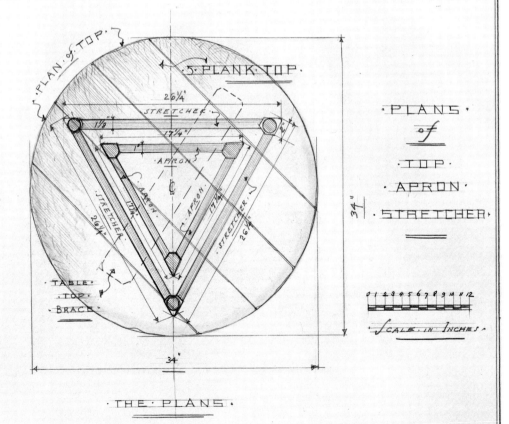

· THE ·
· PILGRIM ·
· CENTURY ·
1700 ·

PLAN of TOP

5 PLANK TOP

26¼

STRETCHER

1⅛"

2"

17¼"

APRON

APRON

17¼

17¼

STRETCHER

APRON

STRETCHER

26¼

26¼

· TABLE ·
· TOP ·
· BRACE ·

34"

34"

· PLANS ·
of
· TOP ·
· APRON ·
· STRETCHER ·

0 1 2 3 4 5 6 7 8 9 10 11 12
· SCALE · IN · INCHES ·

· THE · PLANS ·

· Measured · & · Drawn · by · Lester Margon ·

TAVERN TABLE

Brooklyn Museum   Frank Sherman Benson Fund

All through New England in Colonial times, taverns were the favored gathering places of the populace. Tables with large circular tops and triangular bases permitted many persons to gather about. Furniture of the Pilgrim Century, *circa* 1700, was simple and utilitarian. This tavern table is made of pine and other woods. The turnings are simple and structural and are held in place by straight stretchers. The Brooklyn Museum is well-known for its grouping of American rooms which are furnished in the relative periods. Many of them are models of how such historic rooms should be presented. Whereas the height of this table may seem a bit low, it was not intended for the patrons to sit close to the table but rather to gather about in a large circle. Unable to secure a single piece of wood the required size for the top, note that five planks have been fastened together. The varied effect produced is interesting. As was the custom at the time, wooden pegs served as the method of fastening. Tavern tables like this one reflect the life of the people. Where meeting places were not available in the smaller towns, the tavern served as the meeting place of the community, especially for wayfarers and visitors. The halls rang with good cheer and the ale flowed relentlessly. Paris has its outdoor cafés, Hamburg features the Bier Stube, but in Colonial times the tavern served as the gathering place. Here the news spread rapidly and gossip prevailed. It was a homelike picture that unfortunately has disappeared from the scene.

THE HART ROOM

The Henry Francis du Pont Winterthur Museum

The Hart House was built, *circa* 1670, in Ipswich, Massachusetts. The room illustrated served as a combination sitting room and bedroom. The windows are of leaded glass set in between the studs. The furniture is from New England, with the important court cupboard. The double top extension table is of oak, standing serenely in the center of the room. Facing the brick fireplace are two splendid Carver chairs with rush seats and loose cushions. Of particular interest are the beamed ceiling, the wood panelling and the wide boards of the flooring. In the fireplace are set wrought iron fitments to hold the huge logs. An upright candle bearer and two candlesticks are the only lighting equipment but when the fireplace is burning the entire room is aglow. In the 17th century these family rooms were the most gracious.

TEA TABLE

Museum of the Rhode Island School of Design, Providence

This mahogany tea table is from Newport, Rhode Island, from the middle of the 18th century. It is in the collection of furniture in the Pendleton House of the Rhode Island School of Design Museum in Providence, Rhode Island. The rather rigid cabriole legs terminate in a pointed Dutch foot. There is a raised edge on the top to prevent the fine china from falling off. Below the dish top is a straight apron from which a flared skirt projects to coincide with the line of the cabriole legs. Many of these tables had concealed drawers for silver and pull-outs at the sides to increase the service area. At this Colonial time it was fashionable to serve the new beverage in the living room. Urn stands were also used in combination with the tea tables. Here was one instance when fashion dictated the design and production of a table for a specific purpose. The simplicity of this table is ingratiating. It was made for a definite purpose which it no doubt fulfilled amicably. The making of the tall slender cabriole leg is quite a task, requiring knowledge and skill. When properly fashioned these cabriole legs can be products of pure delight. When they are badly made they can be awesome. The Pendleton House was built in accordance with the general type of Colonial houses in Providence at the middle of the 18th century. It was the gift of Mr. Stephen O. Metcalf to be used as a public museum. The house combines the proportions and decorations of the best houses in Rhode Island.

POLE · SCREEN & CANDLE · SHELF

Metropolitan · Museum · of ART   Circa · 1775

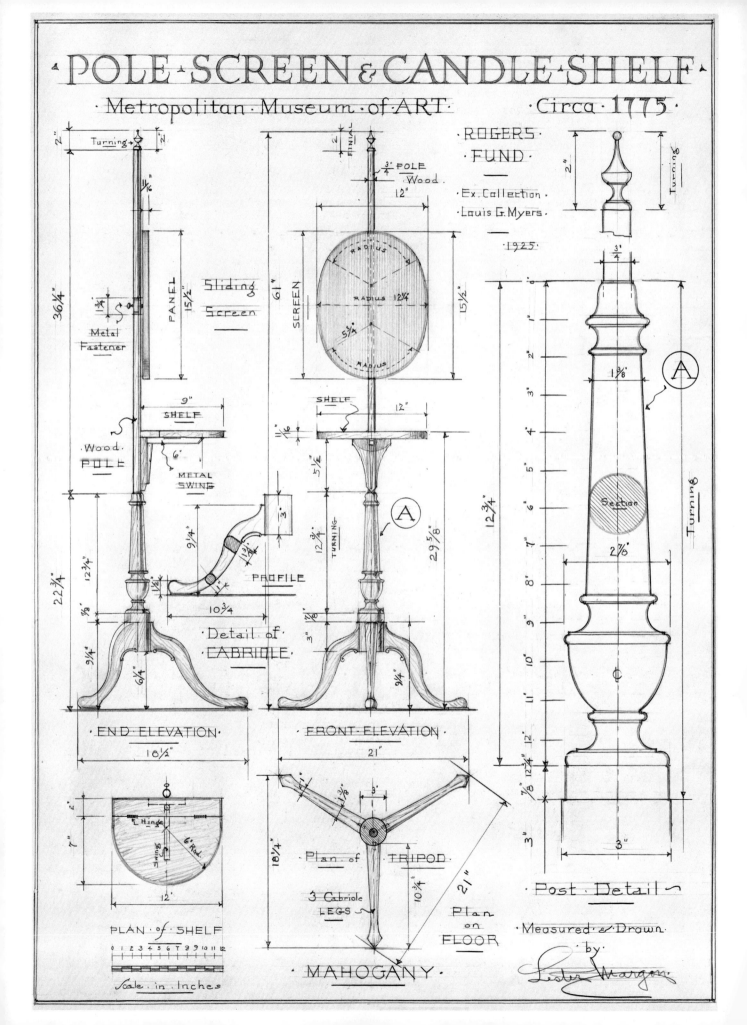

ROGERS · FUND

· Ex. Collection ·
· Louis G. Myers ·

1925

Turning

Sliding
Screen

PANEL

Metal
Fastener

Wood.
POLE

SHELF

METAL
SWING

PROFILE

Detail of
CABRIOLE

· END · ELEVATION ·

FINIAL

POLE
Wood.

SCREEN

RADIUS
RADIUS 12¼
RADIUS

SHELF

TURNING

A

· FRONT · ELEVATION ·

PLAN · of · TRIPOD

3 Cabriole
LEGS

Plan
on
FLOOR

· MAHOGANY ·

PLAN · of · SHELF

E. Hinge

SWING

Scale in Inches

Turning

Section

A

Turning

· Post · Detail ·

· Measured & Drawn ·
· by ·

POLE SCREEN AND CANDLE STAND

Metropolitan Museum of Art   Rogers Fund, 1925

This pole screen and candle stand in mahogany, *circa* 1775, is a purchase from the Rogers Fund, 1925. These stands were a decorative feature, standing beside a chair in the drawing room as a shield against drafts and a protection from possible sparks from the fireplace. On the oval panel a piece of the lady's handiwork, embroidery or a bit of tapestry was displayed. There is a little convenient shelf to hold a candle should the occupant of the chair desire to read. This shelf could be readily dropped when not in use. The tripod base with the cabriole legs is simple and unadorned.

The Classical urn-shaped pedestal is in the best Sheraton tradition. In the Georgian period these incidental pieces of furniture found great favor and ranged from the simplicity of this model to the most elaborate. They were part of the setting of the elegant drawing rooms of the period. Many of them are excellent examples of furniture design. The oval panel could be raised or lowered to suit the caprice of the lady bent on flirtation and conquest. These screens were part of the stage setting against which the play was enacted.

TRUSTEES' OFFICE
Shaker Museum, Old Chatham

In this view of the Trustees' Office at the Shakers' Museum in Old Chatham, New York, the book-keeper's desk is the center of attraction with the high stool. The furniture is from Pleasant Hill, Kentucky. The woods used are chestnut and cherry. In the office are ladder-back rockers, a chest on a stand and a large woven rush basket. All the furniture is simple and utilitarian as was the rule in the Shaker workshops. The commu-nity, with many branches, prospered from 1793 until 1907. There were branches in Kentucky, Maine, New Hampshire, New York, Ohio and Indiana. The Shaker Museum rests in the foothills of the Berkshires. The vast majority of the collec-tions have come direct from the Shaker colonies, but it should be mentioned that the museum has received many valuable and interesting gifts from friends and associates.

HITCHCOCK SIDE CHAIR

Brooklyn Museum   Dick S. Ramsay Fund

Here is a splendid authentic model of a painted and stenciled Sheraton type side chair by Lambert Hitchcock of Hitchcockville, Connecticut, made *circa* 1820. The center wide slat of the back is stenciled with fruit and leaf design decalcomania in metallics. There is considerable gold striping and trim. On the back post is painted an arrow pointing down. The top back rail is turned and shaped, and the rush seat is held firmly by wood pieces and the front seat rail. The legs are most interesting with the wealth of horizontal turned beads as is the front stretcher. This is one of the most original of American chairs. It is distinct and different. These chairs were sold to owners of small houses in New England. Made partly by hand and partly by machine, they were often imitated but never surpassed. Hitchcock chairs are indeed a fresh addition to Americana. This model is in the Brooklyn Museum.

LIST OF ILLUSTRATIONS

(Asterisks indicate photographs accompanied by measured drawings.)

THE SEARCH
FOR BEAUTY

ONE of the strongest urges in man is his desire for immortality. This is the basis of religion and the reason for the existence of all the arts. It is difficult to accept the tenet of the atheist that there is no God and no hereafter. Life is too difficult for us to believe that all this striving is in vain.

Every artistic expression has as its goal the preservation of the artist's perception of beauty, which is a form of immortality for the artist as well. The painter, when he beholds a glorious sunset, is moved to take his brush and paints in hand to preserve the ecstasy of the moment. He is determined to put into permanent form the passing show in the heavens. The musician connects certain tones and turns them into a melody. He is imbued with the desire to set it down, in notes and chords on the staff so that others may share in his creation and be enriched by its beauty. The author, on the other hand, with words at his command, creates characters to populate his story.

How did man find the avenues for his expression? He has had the incentive, from the earliest annals of civilization, to record his activities and ways of life in pictorial forms for posterity. The prehistoric tribes drew designs and incised images on the walls of their caves and colored them with pigments wrung from the earth.

The earliest inscriptions of Thebes were illustrated by pictures. The disk represented the sun and a crescent represented the moon. The Egyptians decorated their sarcophagi in colorful array. The Assyrians modelled their ornaments in low relief and applied colors to the raised surfaces. Greek and Roman sculpture was painted, although little of the coloration remains, due to the ravages of time. It is line and color that breathes life into the arts. This is evidenced in the canvases of the Old Masters, who strove to put their religious fervor into resplendent imagery. In this search for beauty, customs and rituals, beliefs and superstitions, legends and history all play major roles.

But first, in order for man to secure the materials necessary for his existence, there were many conditions and obstacles that had to be overcome. The changing seasons required that man provide some sort of protection for his frail body. He slew wild animals and used the pelts for covering. Then came the need for the construction of some sort of shelter in which to dwell. Man toiled unceasingly, cutting down trees, working the fields, digging into the bowels of the earth to bring forth a variety of metals, as well as stone. The gold and silver was fashioned into ornaments for personal adornment. Most of the lesser materials were used in the construction of a shelter.

A tent or log cabin might have served, but a house is but a shell unless it is fittingly appointed. The needs of living required certain pieces of fixed and movable objects which have become known as furniture. A stump might have been used as a seat and a plank made to serve as a bed. Man was not satisfied with a bundle of sticks and a pile of wood. He began to build furniture that would be beautiful as well as useful, furniture that would contribute materially to his well-being and happiness. As we have come to appreciate that a relationship of one to three or three to five is more pleasing than a ratio of one to two or two to four, by infinite experimentation, trial and error, man arrived at a certain relationship of post and beam that pleased him. He desired to preserve these proportions in what has become known as the Orders of Architecture.

The great kings of Europe were not only the foremost patrons of the arts, but they actually determined the styles during their reigns. The furniture for their palaces and public buildings was often most elaborate and ostentatious. The average person may not build a palace or set a style. His choice of possessions, furniture for instance, is his way of expressing the eternal search for beauty. Even in this there are certain fundamental precepts. Furniture must fulfill the utilitarian demands, afford aesthetic pleasure to the beholder and express the taste and the milieu of the times in which it was created. All furniture, no matter what its use or purpose may entail, should embody a pleasing relationship of line, mass, and proportions. It should be distinct and different while at the same time fulfilling the particular needs for which it is intended.

Contemporary furniture, especially, should be light in weight, firm in structure, simple in design, and should be able to be easily moved about to conform with our present hurried way of living. It should be uncluttered and unaffected, conforming to the modern dictum that form should follow function. A dining room chair, for example, should be of the right height in relation to the table with which it is to be used. It should embody adequate seating propensities, for comfortable eating. A living room chair can be more flexible, and softly upholstered for comfort. A chaise-longue on the other hand, can be rakish in design, embodying the greatest amount of freedom and lounging propensities.

There are universal laws of beauty, which the Greeks caught sight of in the lineation of their temple pediments, and which are evident everywhere if one can perceive them. You may receive the revelation without knowing it, or you may never understand if you live to be as old as Methuselah. It is impossible to set down rules and regulations for the appreciation of beauty. No school can include this in its curriculum and no teacher can impart this knowledge. Only by intuitive observation, persistence and dreaming can one become aware of the beauty that is everywhere. You may catch it in the way a flower bends toward the sun and in the reflections in the still waters of a pool spotted with water-lilies. You may become conscious of the beauty in the defiant straight lines of a skyscraper or in the spreading mass of a Colonial farmhouse. As an attractive girl passes by, her sensuous curves may be an inspiration. The twinkling of myriad stars in the heavens can cast a spell of exaltation.

The same natural laws govern all the arts as they are manifested in the varied phantasmagoria of creation. Man will never cease striving to capture beauty in permanent form, which is perhaps his road to immortality, and at any moment any glimpse of true beauty will prompt him to rally in his search.

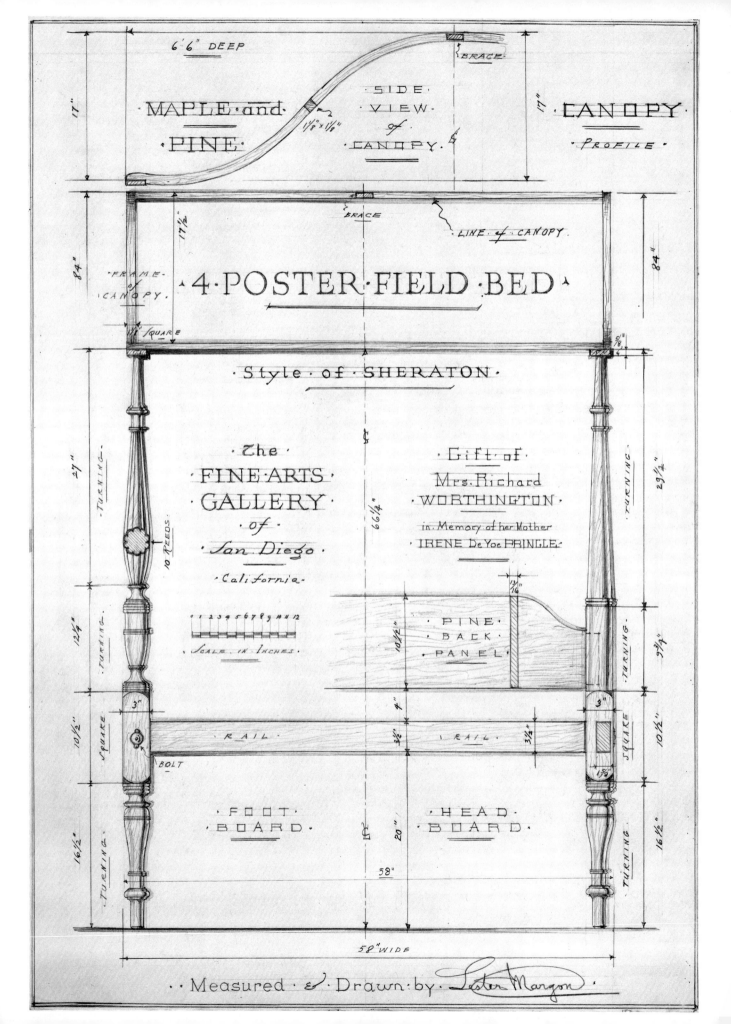

6'6" DEEP

SIDE VIEW of CANOPY

MAPLE and PINE

CANOPY PROFILE

BRACE

1½" × 1½"

17"

17"

17½"

BRACE

LINE of CANOPY

84"

FRAME of CANOPY

·4·POSTER·FIELD·BED·

84"

1½" SQUARE

5/8"

·Style·of·SHERATON·

The FINE·ARTS GALLERY of San Diego ·California·

Gift of Mrs. Richard WORTHINGTON in Memory of her Mother IRENE De Yoe PRINGLE·

27"

TURNING

66¼"

29½"

TURNING

· 1 2 3 4 5 6 7 8 9 10 11 12 ·
· Scale · in · Inches ·

10 REEDS

13/16"

12½"

TURNING

PINE BACK PANEL

9¾"

TURNING

10½"

10½"

SQUARE

3"

RAIL

4"

RAIL

3½"

3"

SQUARE

10½"

BOLT

5/8"

1½"

16½"

TURNING

·FOOT BOARD·

20"

·HEAD BOARD·

16½"

TURNING

58"

58" WIDE

··Measured·&·Drawn·by· Lester Margon·

SHERATON FIELD BED

Fine Arts Gallery, San Diego   Gift of Mrs. Richard Worthington

We may not be inclined to consider the Fine Arts Gallery in Balboa Park, San Diego, California, with its remarkable collection of Western paintings, as a furniture museum. The very startling fact is that it contains a small but formidable collection of Early American furniture. This elegant and refined four-poster field bed is made of maple, *circa* 1800. It is in the Sheraton style, but there are definite heraldings of the approaching Federal period. What made this bed so engrossing are the unusual and exemplary turned and decorated posts. The contrast of the continuous reeding of the bulbous portion with the vertical beading of the urn section below is exceptional and produces a regal effect. The backboard is simple but adequate. The sweep of the structural canopy above affords the necessary support for the most elaborate drapery effects. The bed is in its original finish. These four-poster beds were features in the finest residences of the period. They were often placed on a dais to heighten their importance. Four-poster beds are coming back into fashion again and may be found in the better decorated houses. They do give a pretentiousness and definite importance to an otherwise nondescript bed. There is really nothing grander. Balboa Park is a concentration of public and museum buildings in the Spanish style. The layout is delightful and a visit will prove well worth the trip.

THE HARDENBURGH BEDROOM

The Henry Francis du Pont Winterthur Museum

The Hardenburgh Bedroom, *circa* 1762, near Ker-
honkson, New York, is typical of a Dutch family.
Most of the furnishings are from the Hudson
Valley. Of Continental derivation is the huge
"kas" or two-door cupboard with two drawers
below. It was completely decorated in monochrome grisaille decoration and was sufficiently
spacious to hold everything. Eloquent are the
fiddle-back rush seat arm and side chairs with
turned legs and blunt duck feet. Alongside is

placed the crude cradle which no doubt proved
eminently satisfactory. The spinning wheel is not
set in working position. The four-poster bed is
completely covered with floral linen. On top of
the "kas" are placed a group of colorful pottery
no doubt brought from the homeland. The beamed
ceiling and the wide boarded flooring are typical.
The oriental rug, although not particularly in
keeping, no doubt added a delightful bit of coloring.

BEDROOM WITH FOUR-POSTER BED

Old Sturbridge Village, Sturbridge, Massachusetts

This delightful bedroom featuring the four-poster bed with the copious and eloquently draped canopy with the accompanying bedspread, is from a house in Old Sturbridge Village. The Colonial quality of the setting is outstanding, with the linear design of the rag rug and the striped wallpaper with its insignificant border which also frames the window. The high chest of drawers is magnificent and the shield-back chair is unique, with its raffia woven seat. This is a splendid example of the charm of a true Colonial setting that bespeaks of friendliness and comfort. The towel rack before the window is certainly utilitarian and there is a wash stand partly hidden in this photograph. What a pleasure it is to behold such a room that is reminiscent of life in Colonial America.

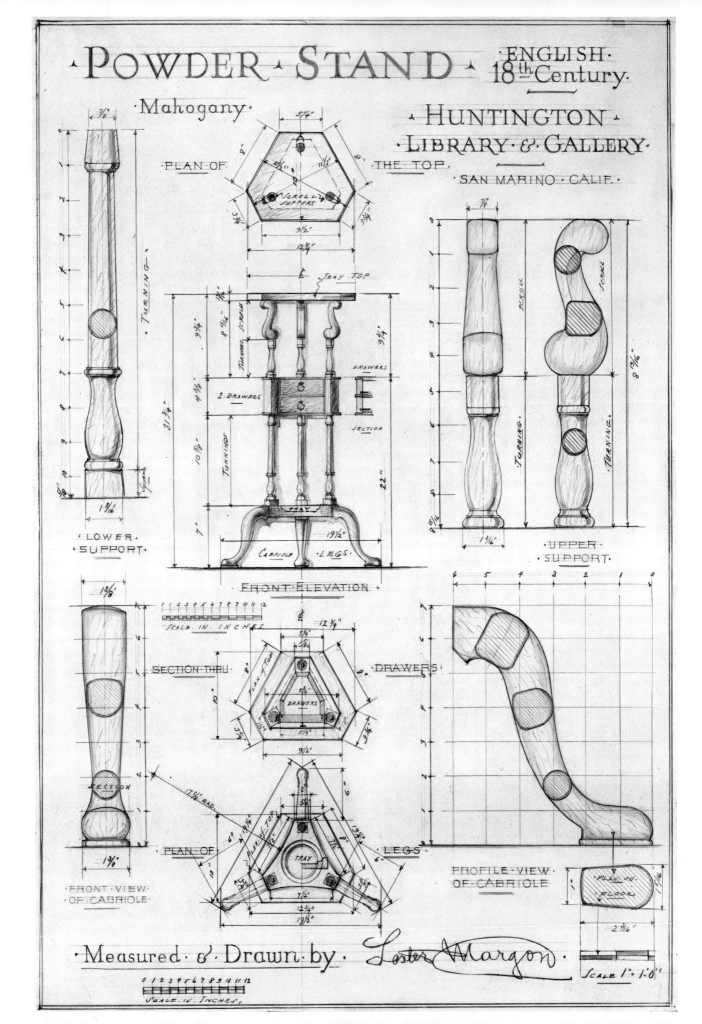

POWDER · STAND

ENGLISH · 18th Century.

Mahogany

PLAN OF   THE · TOP

· HUNTINGTON ·
LIBRARY · & · GALLERY
· SAN · MARINO · CALIF ·

· LOWER ·
· SUPPORT ·

· UPPER ·
· SUPPORT ·

FRONT · ELEVATION

SCALE IN INCHES

SECTION THRU   DRAWERS

PLAN OF   LEGS

· FRONT · VIEW ·
· OF · CABRIOLE ·

· PROFILE · VIEW ·
· OF · CABRIOLE ·

· Measured · & · Drawn · by · Lester Margon

SCALE IN INCHES

SCALE 1" = 1'·0"

POWDER STAND

Henry E. Huntington Art Gallery & Library   Gift of Mrs. Florence M. Quinn, 1944

The Henry E. Huntington Library and Art Gallery in San Marino, California, was completed in 1910 as the residence of the founder. It is now a public treasure with its surrounding extensive grounds, and is one of the great showplaces of California. This mahogany Georgian powder stand is in the Chippendale tradition, and dates from the 18th century. While there are many variations of this type of wig stand, this one is especially delightful, by reason of its restraint and stability. George Washington parked his peruke on such a stand and Martha might have used the bowl stand as a setting for a pitcher cut-out below. Today, wig stands of this high calibre are at a premium. It is a particularly decorative accessory that can be used in the living room, bedroom or library. The making of such a wig stand is indeed a feat. There are so many different members, like the cabriole legs with the duck feet, and the perfect alignment of all the various parts is quite complicated. The turnings are of jewel-like perfection and the scrolled standards are beguiling. The two small drawers at the center give the wig stand strength and provide a place for so many little things. For the cabinetmaker, this small stand presents intriguing features that will well challenge his skill and ingenuity. To produce one will require careful study always keeping in mind the ever changing variations of the sections. Whereas the stand is of the late 18th century it foreshadows the approach of the Victorian period in its unorthodox silhouette and variations.

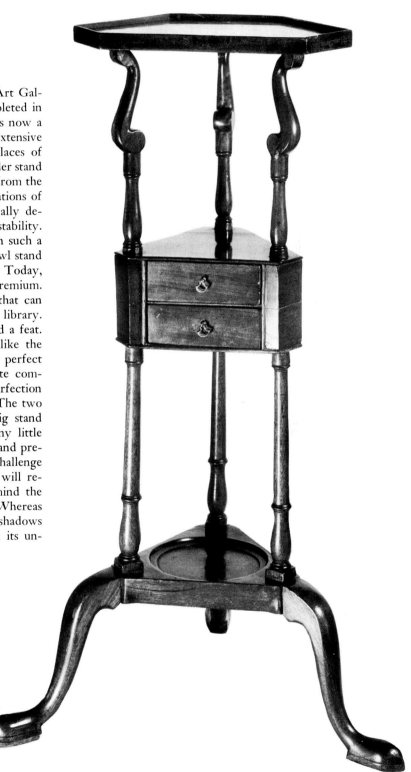

DECORATIVE ARTS GALLERY
Philadelphia Museum of Art

This view of the Decorative Arts Wing, Room #1131 south, is very interesting because it contains so many pieces of Early American furniture. Take for instance the tall Grandfather's clock with the scroll top and the turned finials. The mantlepiece of wood is delightful and the corner cabinet with the open shelves engrossing. Of particular interest are the several Windsor chairs shown which include a loop-back, fan-back, and a comb-back. Notice the well proportioned painted and decorated dresser and the wrought iron lighting fixture. On the walls are hung samplers of intrinsic significance. These bear religious messages and salutations of real worth. They are in a class all their own and especially significant with these Pennsylvania settlers. This gallery is in the Philadelphia Museum of Art.

GRANDFATHER'S CLOCK
The Philadelphia Museum of Art

This Chippendale mahogany musical clock was made by Jacob Gorgas, *circa* 1750-1770. It is Pennsylvania German. While it may not be the most sophisticated in design, workmanship and proportions, it nevertheless has considerable charm. The unique hooded scroll top and the turned finials seem a bit heavy and the apron has too many curvatures. The applied panel on the base is unnecessary. The etched metal dial, made locally, is excellent, with the numerals clearly marked. The waist appears abbreviated, but it is a clock that would fit into the average home. The carving is typical of Lancaster but the top appears heavy. The panelled door with the circular window is for one to make sure that the pendulum is swinging.

CHEST·ON·A·STAND·

·METROPOLITAN·MUSEUM·OF·ART·

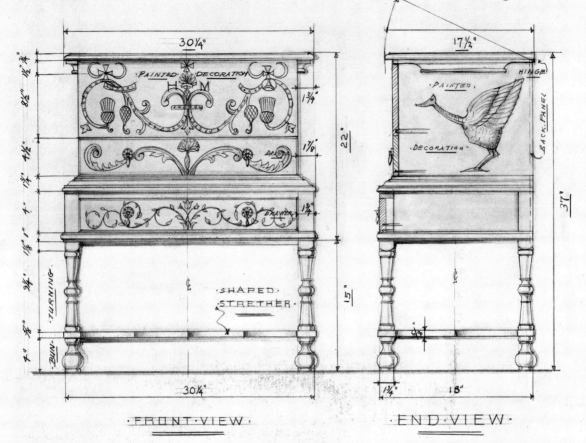

·FRONT·VIEW·   ·END·VIEW·

·1700· PAINTED·&·DECORATED·

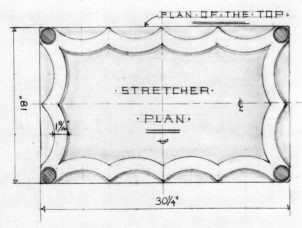

·PLAN·OF·THE·TOP·

STRETCHER·
PLAN·

·PLANS·of·TOP·&·STRETCHER·

·LEGEND·

Whitewood·Painted·
&·Decorated·BROWN·
with·RED·WHITE·&·
BLACK·Decorations·

·SCALE·IN·INCHES·

·Measured·&·Drawn·by·Testa Margon·

CHEST ON A STAND

Metropolitan Museum of Art, New York   Gift of Mrs. Russell Sage, 1910

There are very few well designed and finely executed examples of painted furniture as early as 1700. Most of them are so crudely executed that they might have been done by children. However, this chest on a stand is an exemplary exception. It is indeed a regal conception, elegant in execution. While it is reminiscent of the style of William and Mary, the freshness of treatment makes it definitely American. The freedom of the scrolls and the formality of the layout, with the family crest and the initials of the owner proudly emblazoned, make it a piece of distinction. Most

amusing is the painting of the fowl on the side. It appears ready to take off. The chest is painted in a deep brown and the decoration is brought out in red, white and black. The upper part is a chest with a hinged top, probably intended to hold a blanket. There are two long drawers below. The stand itself is very interesting with the odd-shaped legs held in place by a shaped stretcher. Altogether it is a most engaging piece. It was a gift of Mrs. Russell Sage in 1909. This lady has given so many excellent pieces to the American Wing.

PAINTED PINE CHEST

The Brooklyn Museum   H. Randolph Lever Fund

This pine chest is another fine example of the free-painted decoration of the early settlers. The chest is from Taunton, Massachusetts, *circa* 1710-1725. The scrolls are painted in ivory on a dark brown ground and the flowers are outlined in white with black petals. The top is hinged to allow for the placement of blankets and there is one long drawer below. These peasant painted chests are so delightful because they are the nat-ural expression of the designer. The rhythm of the scrolls is so well calculated that they present a wealth of decoration covering the entire front elevation. Indeed the scroll decoration is well planned to permit the flowers to attain their wonted prominence. These peasant painted chests are rare and much sought after. Their enchant-ment is undeniable. They are the untutored ex-pression of the joy of natural surroundings.

A CHILD'S CHEST

Art Institute of Chicago

This pine painted and decorated chest is probably by Robert Crosman of Taunton, Massachusetts, *circa* 1707-1799. It is a rare and delightful piece of child's furniture. It is small, measuring only 20″ high x 22″ wide. The top is hinged, possibly to hold the toys that had been scattered about the house during the day. There is one long drawer below. The initials of the proud owner are emblazoned across the escutcheon plate. What a joy!

When fancy plays a part in the world of a child, what daydreams may be envisioned. Look at the painted decoration. A fantastic tree spreads its branches to shield the little chickadees. In the dream world of a child there is no need for realism. If there were only more such pieces of furniture for children to cheer the world, how happy we would be!

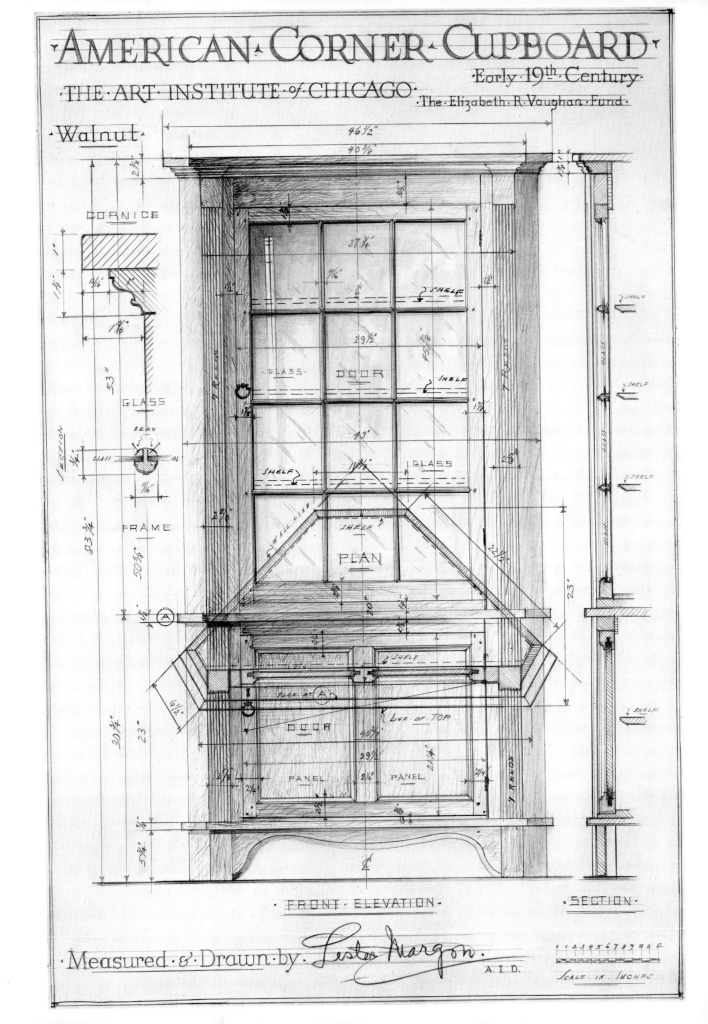

AMERICAN · CORNER · CUPBOARD

THE · ART · INSTITUTE · of · CHICAGO

Early · 19th · Century

The · Elizabeth · R · Vaughan · Fund

Walnut

CORNICE

GLASS

BEAD

GLASS   GL

FRAME

GLASS   DOOR

SHELF

SHELF

SHELF   GLASS

PLAN

DOOR

PANEL   PANEL

LINE · of · TOP

7 REEDS

7 REEDS

SHELF

SHELF

SHELF

7 REEDS

· FRONT · ELEVATION ·

· SECTION ·

· Measured · & · Drawn · by · Lester Margon ·

A.I.D.

SCALE · IN · INCHES

CORNER CUPBOARD

Art Institute of Chicago   *Bequest of Elizabeth R. Vaughan Fund*

Another purchase from the Elizabeth R. Vaughan Fund of the Art Institute of Chicago, this corner cupboard was made in Eastern Ohio in the early 19th century. It is fashioned of walnut. The Colonial corner cupboards became a part of the architectural styling of the rooms and in this capacity lent dignity to the surroundings. They struck the note for the other pieces of furniture in the setting. Besides the architectural aspects the corner cupboard offered display space for the fine china and glass that was being collected at this time. The lower compartment permitted storage. Many of the glass-enclosed areas were painted, adding a note of color to the ensemble. Some of these cabinets were treated with Japanese lacquer and finely decorated. The simple reeded pilasters at the sides are the sole decorative motif but this is masterfully conceived to produce a pleasing austerity. The unadorned moulded cornice is just right. The lack of extraneous detail makes this corner cupboard so attractive in the modern sense of appraisement. Of course, it is the delicate wooden divisions of the glass door that make it so impressive and give proper majesty to the elevation. Inside are three movable shelves. Cabinets like this fit snugly into the corner. Modern innovations in these pieces include the substitution of glass shelves, with indirect lighting concealed near the top.

WILLIAMSBURG

The Colonial Capitol   View of the Governor's Palace, Photograph by Bill Uetzmann

Although Williamsburg never attained the commercial importance of other neighboring towns, its position as the social and political center of Virginia was unquestioned. In April 1776, when the Burgesses decided that liberty without independence was impossible, Virginia broke off ties with Great Britain. In 1781 Cornwallis entered Williamsburg and levied great damage upon the community. Three months later, when Washing-ton moved on to Yorktown, he struck the decisive blow that won the Colonists' freedom. Whereas much of the furniture in the Governor's Palace was imported from England, many pieces of American made furniture may be seen in the Raleigh Tavern. This famous inn was frequented by Washington, Jefferson and members of the most prominent Virginia families.

FORMAL DINING ROOM
GOVERNOR'S PALACE

Colonial Williamsburg, Williamsburg, Virginia

This handsome formal dining room was used on official occasions. The huge table and the accompanying side chairs are probably of English origin although some of the furniture may have been made by Williamsburg cabinetmakers. However, the furniture fits graciously into the Colonial environment. The curtains are original – 17th century – of cut velvet in dark green and ivory. The English silver wall sconces are of the William III period and the silver epergne, dated 1759, was made in England by William Cripps. Above the carved and gilded console table hangs a Chippendale style looking-glass. Above the marble mantlepiece is placed a man's portrait in an elaborately carved frame. The Classical design of the interior becomes a fitting background for festive occasions. The several silver candlesticks are unique and the parade of figurines on top of the mantle engrossing.

· SECRETARY · BOOKCASE · 1790 ·

· METROPOLITAN · MUSEUM · OF · ART ·

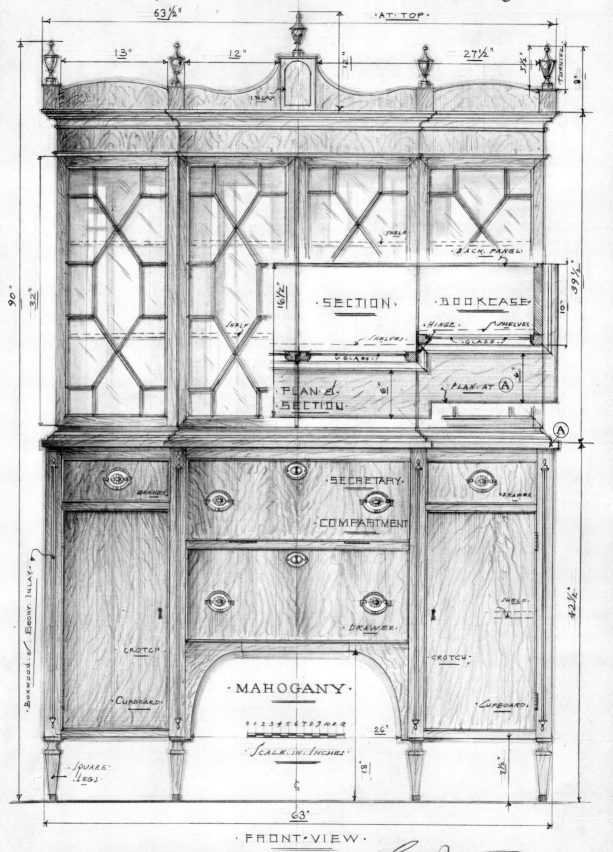

· AT · TOP ·

63½"

13"   12"   12"   27½"   5½"

·INLAY·

·TURNING·

8"

90"   32"   39½"

·SHELF·

·BACK·PANEL·

16½"   · SECTION ·   · BOOKCASE ·

10"

·SHELVES·   ·HINGE·   ·SHELVES·

·GLASS·   ·GLASS·

· PLAN · &   6"   · PLAN · AT Ⓐ

· SECTION ·

Ⓐ

·DRAWER·   · SECRETARY ·   ·DRAWER·

· COMPARTMENT ·

42½"

·BOXWOOD · & · EBONY · INLAY·

·SHELF·

·DRAWER·

·CROTCH·   ·CROTCH·

· MAHOGANY ·   ·CUPBOARD·

·CUPBOARD·

0 1 2 3 4 5 6 7 8 9 10 11 12   26"

· SCALE · IN · INCHES ·

18"   ·SQUARE·   7½"

·LEGS·

63"

· FRONT · VIEW ·

· Measured · & · Drawn · by · Lester Margon ·

SECRETARY BOOKCASE

Metropolitan Museum of Art   Gift of Mrs. Russell Sage, 1909

This Hepplewhite Secretary Bookcase, *circa* 1790-1800, is one of the grandest pieces of this period. The bookcase top is enclosed in glass with applied geometric trellis work. This piece is of distinctly American design. The proportions are excellent and the space divisions so cleverly contrived that the great mass is cleverly camouflaged. The crest is graceful in its delineation. The crotch mahogany is not flamboyant but richly figured to produce the proper dignity. The brass pulls and escutcheon plates are delightful. The square tapered legs are just right for this piece. The raised bead around the drawers and cupboards produces the needed accents. The secretary compartment, when opened, reveals the usual small drawers and cubby-holes. This piece was undoubtedly made in Salem, Massachusetts, for it resembles a similar secretary bookcase made by Edmund Johnson who produced the highest quality of furniture in Salem. Our piece is in the American Wing of the Metropolitan Museum of Art, that treasure house of American furniture.

PARLOR OF THE PRENTIS HOUSE

Shelburne Museum, Shelburne, Vermont

Photo by Taylor & Dull, New York (Courtesy of Antiques *Magazine)*

The Shelburne Museum was established in 1947 by Electra Havermeyer Webb. She gave to the museum impeccable taste and the knowledge of a lifetime of collecting. Authorities have called the Shelburne Museum one of the finest in America. It is indeed the museum of the American spirit. Occupying forty-five acres, it comprises thirty-five buildings and the *S.S. Ticonderoga.* The parlor of the Prentis house was opened in 1955. It is the earliest architectural unit now assembled on the museum grounds. It is furnished with a notable collection of New England furniture, *circa* 1710. Shown in this photograph are two Spanish-foot side chairs attributed to John Gaines of New Hampshire. The cushions are contemporary moquette in green and gold. The Prentis House has character and distinction, containing all the original woodwork.

THE EAST CHAMBER – THE PRENTIS HOUSE

Shelburne Museum, Shelburne, Vermont

Photo by Taylor & Dull, New York (Courtesy of Antiques *Magazine)*

The East Chamber of the Prentis House is furnished with items from the 17th century that were made in New England. Above the William and Mary lowboy hangs a small looking-glass with beadwork panels and a carved wooden frame. The side chair with the Spanish feet, turned stretchers and pierced carved cresting of the back has a rush seat. It is attributed to John Gaines of Portsmouth, New Hampshire. He is known to have made furniture "handsomely and faithfully." Examples of his work may be seen at the Winterthur Museum and the Metropolitan Museum of Art. Before the window stands a circular-top table holding a treasure box and two candlesticks. Not shown, is a New England bed with an indigo blue quilted bedspread.

LIST OF ILLUSTRATIONS

(Asterisks indicate photographs accompanied by measured drawings.)

LADDER-BACK CHAIR*
Wadsworth Atheneum, Hartford
LADDER-BACK CHAIR
Art Institute of Chicago
SLAT-BACK ARMCHAIR
Metropolitan Museum of Art
PRETZEL-BACK SIDE CHAIR*
Wadsworth Atheneum, Hartford
PRETZEL-BACK ARMCHAIR
Winterthur Museum
GEORGIAN SIDE CHAIR
Victoria and Albert Museum, London
WING CHAIR*
Essex Institute, Salem
THE BLACKWELL PARLOR
Winterthur Museum
MEMORIAL HALL
Philadelphia Museum
PHILADELPHIA SIDE CHAIR*
Detroit Institute of Arts
QUEEN ANNE SIDE CHAIR
Winterthur Museum
PAINTED ARMCHAIR
Winterthur Museum
GEORGIAN WING CHAIR*
Huntington Art Gallery and Library
THE TAPPAHANNOCK ROOM
Winterthur Museum
CHIPPENDALE WING CHAIR
Philadelphia Museum of Art
CONNECTICUT SIDE CHAIR*
Art Institute of Chicago
"SHOEMAKER" ARMCHAIR
Philadelphia Museum of Art
CHIPPENDALE STYLE SIDE CHAIR
Metropolitan Museum of Art

AMERICAN SIDE CHAIR*
Metropolitan Museum of Art
CHIPPENDALE STYLE SIDE CHAIR
Victoria and Albert Museum, London
SHIELD-BACK SIDE CHAIR
Metropolitan Museum of Art
LYRE-BACK SIDE CHAIR*
Detroit Institute of Arts
DUNCAN PHYFE SIDE CHAIR
Cooper-Hewitt Museum, New York
WAINSCOT ARMCHAIR
Winterthur Museum
FAN-BACK WINDSOR CHAIR*
Art Institute of Chicago
LOOP-BACK WINDSOR CHAIR
Art Institute of Chicago
WINDSOR SETTEE
Winterthur Museum
COMB-BACK WINDSOR CHAIR*
Fine Arts Gallery, San Diego
THE HARVEST ROOM
Shelburne Museum, Vermont
COMB-BACK WINDSOR CHAIR
Art Institute of Chicago
WRITING-ARM WINDSOR CHAIR*
Metropolitan Museum of Art
KITCHEN OF THE VERMONT HOUSE
Shelburne Museum, Vermont
INFANT'S WINDSOR HIGH CHAIR
Brooklyn Museum, New York
HITCHCOCK ROCKER*
Brooklyn Museum, New York
SPINDLE-BACK ROCKER
Shakers' Museum, Old Chatham, New York
SHAKER ROCKER
Cooper-Hewitt Museum, New York

CHAIRS

4

THE chair is a symbol of the way in which we live and conduct ourselves. This makes it one of the most important features of furniture
design. Playing a major role in the daily lives of our people as it does,
its development follows the history of our country. Although the chair is
the most difficult task for the designer, there is a profusion of good chairs
that proves the skill and knowledge of furniture makers.

Man, by reason of his anatomical structure, is capable of only
three lasting positions: standing erect, lying down, and sitting. All other
intermediate positions require special muscular control and cannot be of
lasting duration. Since this is true, man has fashioned a structure, known
as a chair, to receive the body in a sitting position. With the possible
exception of the bed, the chair is the most useful piece of furniture yet
created.

When a person sits in a chair, there are three areas of bodily con-
tact: seat, back, and arms, but the size, shape, structure and design of a
chair will depend largely on the particular services for which it is intended. History has played an important part in its evolution. Chairs
during the Middle Ages and the Renaissance were in reality thrones. The
Baroque and the Rococo emphasized balance and harmony in the design
for comfort. Chairs of the three Louis periods searched for elegance incorporating Classic influences. The Empire regime produced chairs that
again resembled the throne.

The variety of chairs, and their diversity in type and design is
infinite. It would be impossible, even in drawings and photographs, to

collect any percentage of the different types of chairs that have been made during the last three centuries. The number of chairs recorded since the dawn of civilization is legion.

In the British Museum may be seen bas-reliefs showing that chairs were used by the Egyptians. In the Old Testament there are references to seating pieces. The records of Thebes show examples of chairs with feet of animal claw design. The Assyrians incorporated the heads of animals in their chairs. A bronze throne was found in the ruins of Nimrod's palace. Depicted on Greek and Roman vases of as early as the 6th Century B.C. may be seen persons reclining on couches, with stools at their feet.

The epitome of purity of design was classical Greece. With the fall of the Roman Empire demoralization set in over Europe and until the Middle Ages the legend of furniture is uncertain and obscure. Little is known until the capture of Constantinople in 1452. However, a fine example of the period of heroic Christian struggles against feudalism is the chair of St. Peter in Rome. In Westminster Abbey stands the Coronation Chair of Edward I, dating from 1292, made of oak in Gothic design. It was at that time that the church dominated the lives of the populace, and there were at bedsides "prie-dieu" settles with seats that lifted up to receive devotional tracts.

The development of the chair is so closely related to the manners and the customs of the people that it underwent many changes to conform with the varying concepts of comfort and utility. In the Middle Ages chairs were practically unknown in the homes, and a chair was the seat of dignity and authority reserved for the use of the master of the house and for special guests. All others either sprawled on benches or remained standing. During the Renaissance chairs were of goodly proportions with much carving and the addition of upholstery. The Restoration brought greater formality, with the use of rich textiles. The Jacobean and Elizabethan periods used oak and favored the straight line. Queen Anne preferred the curvilinear, similar to the prevailing French models. The use of mahogany as a cabinet wood was introduced during the Georgian period.

The first quarter of the 18th century saw the manufacture of a Provincial type of chair that became popular as the "Windsor." Its origin is uncertain and the exact location of the original factory is not known. In America it was probably made in Philadelphia *circa* 1725. There were many varieties of this chair, featuring solid wooden seats, scooped and shaped for comfort. A variety of woods was used. Most of these chairs had turned legs and stretchers, with backs consisting of spindles held in place by top rails or bends.

In 1754 Thomas Chippendale published "The Gentleman & Cabinet-maker's Director." This book added greatly to his prestige and popularity. His best work was in the design of chairs, which he understood thoroughly. He was a master of carving and used it exclusively for ornamentation. There were Gothic, Chinese, and Irish Chippendale, and backs of chairs featuring fanciful ribband intricacies.

George Hepplewhite added much grace and dignity to his chair designs, which included shield and oval back designs, with tapered front legs. Thomas Sheraton favored the square back. Many of his chairs had pierced center panels incorporating a vase-shaped central splat, carved and ornamented. In 1791 he published "The Cabinet-maker and Upholsterer's Drawing Book," which to this day is the source for copying by furniture manufacturers. Among his designs were banister-back chairs. The later Sheraton designs were painted and decorated and might be considered "fancy" chairs.

American furniture during these periods followed rather closely the work being done on the Continent. However, the American designers took a fresh look at the situation and adapted the foreign models to the requirements of the new country. This often produced work that surpassed the European.

During the Reign of Louis XIV, France became the cultural center of the world. Its elegance rivaled the extravagance of the Roman Empire. For the enormous rooms of the palaces and public buildings, large scale furniture was necessary. This was especially true in the design of chairs, for the ladies' paniered skirts required adequate seating arrangements. Compass curves and richly carved pierced aprons on consoles predominated. This was accomplished under the direction of Charles Lebrun, the director of decoration appointed by the king. Louis XV favored the assymetrical in design. Many of his chairs were fragile. His reign was marked by sentimentality with aspects of the effeminate. The attitude of Louis XVI was quite different. He brought back the symmetrical with emphasis on the Classical, influenced by the current excavation being undertaken at Pompeii and Herculaneum.

Napoleon Bonaparte inaugurated a new period in furniture design and decoration known as the "Empire," enlisting the services of the architects Perçier and Fontaine. They bolstered the emperor's desire for the glorification of his victories on the battlefield. The chairs of the Empire period were massive and generally made of mahogany. Many of them assumed the aspect of a throne. The austerity of the highly polished mahogany was enlivened by the application of ormolu for decoration. Many of these pieces were of allegorical design. The style continued in favor until *circa* 1840 and influenced much of the furniture being made throughout Europe and America.

You may ask why so much stress and emphasis are put on the design of chairs. The truth is that chairs are the most significant contribution to any period. To appreciate the design of a chair is to know the worth of all the related pieces of furniture. Every line, every curve, every inclination is an important factor. An incorrect slant, an error in the plan, a false rhythm in the way the back flows into the seat — any of these defects may defeat the design of a chair. It has been said that "a good chair is worth its weight in gold." Of all the domestic pleasures there is none greater than sitting in a comfortable chair. It not only supports the body but induces relaxation and affords a sense of well-being. All the effort and study that a designer has put into the design of a chair is well rewarded when a client sits in the chair and smiles contentedly in recognition and appreciation of a task well done. There is no greater praise for the designer than this.

SIDE CHAIR FROM THEBES
The Louvre, Paris, France

The first and second epochs of Thebes, 3200-2780 B.C., were known as photodynamic. The Egyptians produced decorative and household objects with exceptional skill and perception. Their work included jewelry in silver and gold and translucent stone, and furniture. The Egyptians' innate sense of proportion gave their work a concordant balance that is exceptional for that early age. This is particularly evident in the design of this side chair now in the Louvre in Paris. The sophisticated curve of the back, the discreet placing of the lotus decorations, and the inclusion of the animal feet in the design give the chair distinction and character. The way the wood of the back is used to further the design, and the inclusion of the repetitious border at the top are excellent. The woven leather seat permits seat flexibility. All in all, it is a wonderful chair.

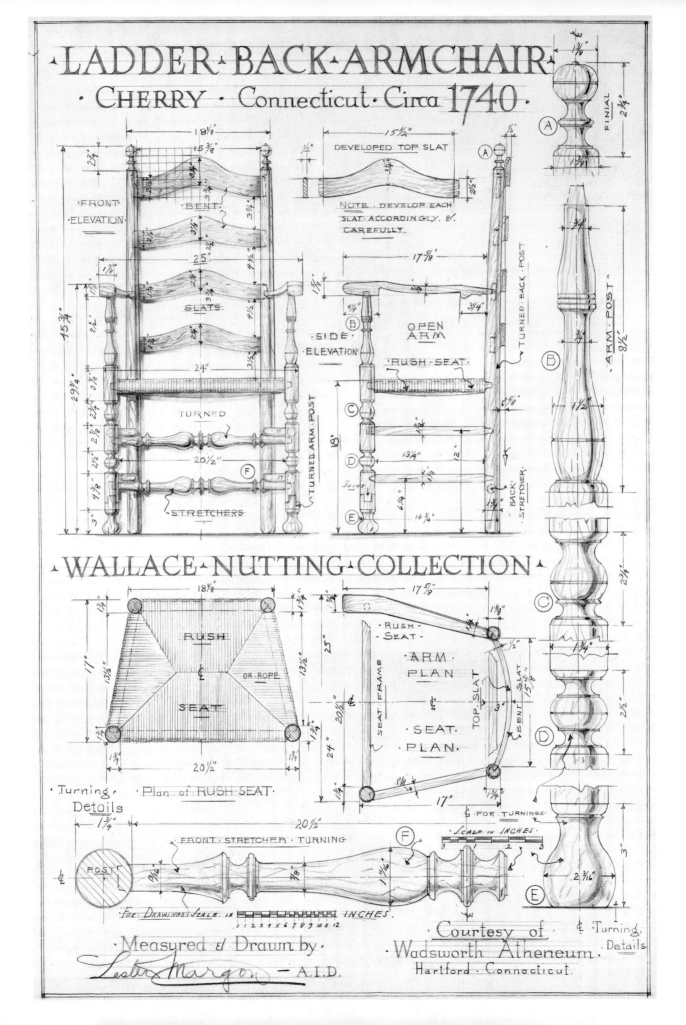

LADDER·BACK·ARMCHAIR·
·CHERRY· Connecticut·Circa 1740·

WALLACE·NUTTING·COLLECTION

·Measured & Drawn by·

Lester Margon — A.I.D.

·Courtesy of·
Wadsworth Atheneum·
Hartford·Connecticut·

LADDER-BACK ARMCHAIR

Wadsworth Atheneum, Hartford, Connecticut   *Wallace Nutting Collection*

In the Wadsworth Atheneum in Hartford, Connecticut, is a choice selection of the Wallace Nutting Collection of furniture. This ladder-back chair was built *circa* 1740. A combination of woods was used in the making of these chairs, including cherry, pine, adair, maple and oak. In fact, whatever woods were available were used. The rush seat lent itself to greater comfort. Before going any further in the analysis of this chair, it will be interesting to note a bit of bibliography: Rev. Wallace Nutting was a clergyman who turned to photography, writing, and the collecting of antique furniture because of ill health. His books, "State Beautiful" and "Clock Book" remain the standard works on the subjects. His "Furni-

ture Treasury" contains some 5,000 photographs of furniture and utensils which he had collected. This type of ladder-back chair resembles closely one belonging to William Penn, which he brought over from England. However, the model shown has greater reserve. The slope of the arms creates the stately seating propensity. The bending of the slats of the ladder back is of the utmost importance. Note that they are all different in size, bend, and line. Of course, the foremost challenge in producing this type of chair is the intricacy and beauty of the turned posts and stretchers. Their rhythm is infinite, their grace beyond bounds. This chair is a masterpiece.

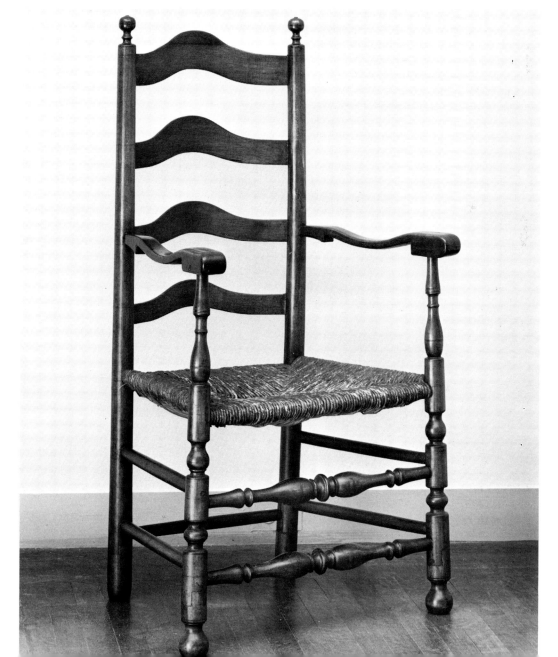

LADDER-BACK ARMCHAIR

The Art Institute of Chicago   Sewell L. Avery Fund (purchase)

Coming from New York or Connecticut, this maple and ash ladder-back armchair was made *circa* 1740. It is painted black and has a rush seat. The front and back posts are turned, with finials. The four slats are of varied sizes and shapes, with different bends. The stretcher turnings are simple and rigid. This is an attractive chair, but a little on the heavy side. As the century progressed the chairs became lighter. Of special interest is the lower turning below the arm support, between the front and the back posts. This is most unusual. Chairs like this were to be found in farmhouses in the rural districts, and this one is definitely provincial in character. It is in reality a combination of the Carver and the slat-back chairs. This model is in the collection of the Art Institute of Chicago.

SLAT-BACK ARMCHAIR

Metropolitan Museum of Art   Gift of Mrs. Russell Sage, 1909

One of the earliest types of chair from the Pilgrim Century, this slat-back armchair dates from *circa* 1650-1700. Made of pine and ash, its very simplicity is beguiling. The front legs and the back posts are turned, with an interesting finial on top of the back posts. The three shaped slats are of similar design but of different widths. They are all slightly bent. The rush seat is held firmly between the front legs and the back posts. In this instance it is softened by the application of a cushion seat. The stretchers are simple, as is the one serving as the arm brace. Despite its evident simplicity, this armchair is prepossessing. It speaks well of the honesty and straightforwardness of these early settlers in New England. This armchair is in the American Wing of the Metropolitan Museum of Art.

PRETZEL·BACK·CHAIR·

WADSWORTH·ATHENEUM·HARTFORD·

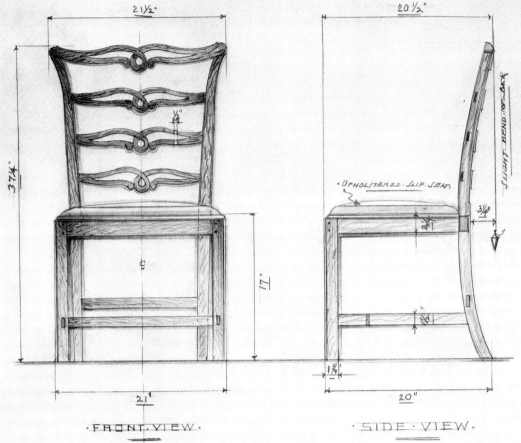

21½"

20½"

37¼"

17"

UPHOLSTERED·SLIP·SEAT·

SLIGHT·BEND·OF·BACK

3¼"

21"

20"

1 5/16"

· FRONT·VIEW ·

· SIDE·VIEW ·

0 1 2 3 4 5 6 7 8 9 10 11 12

· SCALE·IN·INCHES ·

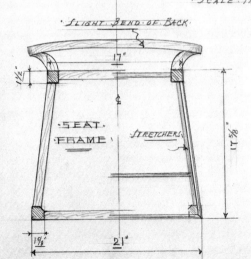

· SLIGHT·BEND·OF·BACK·

17"

1½"

· SEAT·
FRAME ·

· STRETCHERS·

17 5/8"

1 9/16"

21"

· THE·PLAN ·

· Attributed·to·
ELIPHALET·CHAPIN·

—

· CHERRY·&·PINE·

—

· 1741~1807·

Measured · & · Drawn · by · · Lester Margon.

PRETZEL-BACK SIDE CHAIR

Wadsworth Atheneum, Hartford, Connecticut   *Gift from the Estate of Mrs. Horace B. Clark*

The more literate would probably call this model a slat-back side chair. However, the term "pretzel" is more descriptive of this particular design. This is in fact one of the most popular chairs of the period and was made by many designers with various interpretations. Dating from *circa* 1770, this side chair is made of cherry and pine. It is attributed to Eliphalet Chapin, who hailed from East Windsor, Connecticut. He served his apprenticeship in Enfield, followed by four years of training in Philadelphia. Eliphalet Chapin's furniture shows definite influences of this training. He worked almost entirely in cherry and produced much beautiful furniture. His chairs were particularly successful and found a ready market. However, his fame may be directly associated with his chests-on-chests, and highboys with fluted columns at the corners and distinctive cabriole legs terminating in ball-and-claw feet. He occasionally used inlay. Examples of Eliphalet Chapin's work may be seen in the Garvin Collection at Yale University, at Williams College, and in the collection of the Wadsworth Atheneum in Hartford. While not considered one of the foremost cabinet-makers, he was one of the best.

PRETZEL-BACK ARMCHAIR

The Henry Francis du Pont Winterthur Museum

Ephraim Haines and Benjamin Trotter were associate cabinetmakers. Both were known for the making of the so-called "pretzel-back chairs." These designs were developed from English models. Working in Philadelphia, Ephraim Haines and Benjamin Trotter made many variations of this type of chair. In New England at this time, the simple version of the ladder-back chair was losing favor. The slat-back chair also had not been so popular since the Pilgrim Century. Of course, these chairs are definitely of the Chippendale style, but so simplified as to warrant calling them American. It is fortunate for the cabinetmaker who can feel the trend of the times. Looking at this model carefully, we can see that it is really Chippendale in line, detail, and manifestation. This chair is in the Henry Francis du Pont Winterthur Museum.

GEORGIAN CHAIR
Victoria and Albert Museum, London

This walnut side chair is carved and in part veneered. It is one of a set in the collection of the Victoria and Albert Museum in London, made *circa* 1730-1735. Early Georgian furniture was generally made of mahogany. This chair is an exception. As seen in the photograph, it features the curvilinear line with a good amount of carving. Whereas the general silhouette is of the Queen Anne style, the interpretation here has been elaborated with an excessive amount of carving. The cabriole legs are fashioned with multifid carving at the knee descending to the ball-and-claw-feet. It all seems to be a little too much. However, that was the tendency at the time, under the leadership of Swan and Kent. The designers seemed to put all they knew into their work. Still, this chair is truly elegant.

WING·CHAIR·American·1765·

·ESSEX·INSTITUTE··SALEM·MASS.

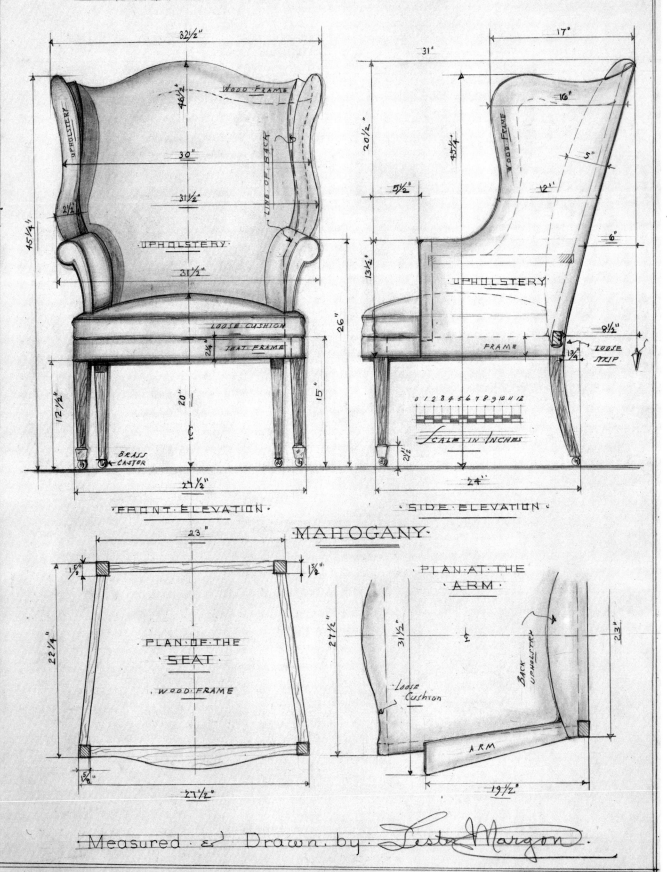

·FRONT·ELEVATION·

·SIDE·ELEVATION·

MAHOGANY·

PLAN·OF·THE SEAT

·WOOD·FRAME·

PLAN·AT·THE ARM

·Measured·&·Drawn·by·Lester Margon·

WING CHAIR

Essex Institute, Salem, Massachusetts

From the great collection of Colonial furniture at the Essex Institute in Salem, Massachusetts, this superb wing chair was selected for study. It is one of the most typical American seating pieces. It is the epitome of comfort and elegance. While the chair shows the influence of the Chippendale style, nowhere else but in this country could it have been made. The date is *circa* 1765. The square tapered legs are fitted with brass wheeled casters. There is a loose cushion to fit snugly about the frame. The flare of the arms is superlative and the contour of the entire chair is beyond compare.

It is indeed a pleasure to behold such a splendid wing chair of the Colonial period. In the fashionable living rooms of the times such a wing chair might have been set before the fire. Its well-shaped upholstered wings would shield the occupant from any possible draft or sparks from the fire. Such chairs were often upholstered in rich damasks, needle-point, brocatelles or linens of fine weave. At this time the use of chintz was favored. Note that the wings are flamboyant but the front of the arms is straight, affording a contrasting feature.

THE BLACKWELL PARLOR

The Henry Francis du Pont Winterthur Museum

The Blackwell House was originally located at No. 224 Pine Street, Philadelphia. The furniture in the parlor represents the finest craftsmanship of the Revolutionary period in America. The formal elegance of this living room is phenomenal. It is the last word in convenience. The two chairs standing beside the mahogany console table are attributed to Benjamin Randolph, one of the foremost cabinetmakers and carvers of the period.

Between the windows hangs a white and gold Chippendale mirror. The crystal chandelier is of Irish cut glass. The pie-crust table is one of the finest. Nearby stands an inviting winged easy chair covered in precious brocade. Especially noteworthy is the interior trim, fine in detail and splendidly executed. This gracious parlor befits those who once occupied it.

MEMORIAL HALL

Pennsylvania Museum, Memorial Hall, Philadelphia

This is a splendid view of the galleries in the Pennsylvania Museum, Memorial Hall, in Philadelphia, which are notable for the Colonial interpretation of the Doric style for the interiors. This creates a formidable backdrop for the display of the unrivaled selection of American furniture of the Georgian period. Each piece shown is a genuine treasure and certainly shows brilliant selection. Most museums of necessity have to crowd their possessions into a limited space. This is not the case in Memorial Hall. The architects have wisely permitted the background to augment the importance of the objects shown. The oriental rugs, scattered about, add much to the eloquence of the ensembles. The settee, the mirror above, and the armchair in the further gallery are all magnificent pieces.

· PHILADELPHIA · SIDE · CHAIR ·

· THE · DETROIT · INSTITUTE · OF · ARTS ·

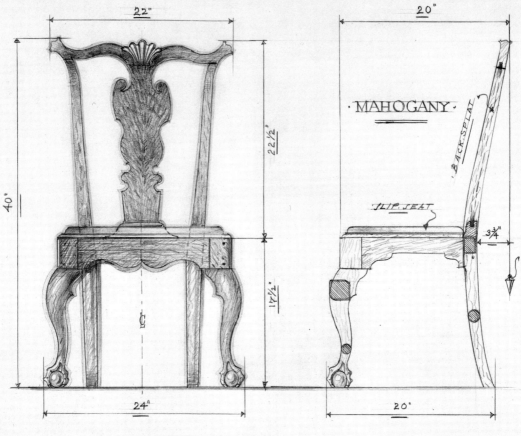

· FRONT · VIEW ·

· SIDE · VIEW ·

· MAHOGANY ·

BACKSPLAT

SLIP SEAT

3¾"

22"

40'

22½"

17½"

24"

20'

20'

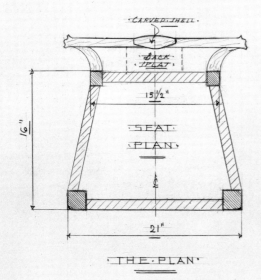

· CARVED · SHELL ·

· BACK · SPLAT ·

15½"

· SEAT ·

· PLAN ·

16"

21"

· THE · PLAN ·

0 1 2 3 4 5 6 7 8 9 10 11 12
· SCALE · IN · INCHES ·

· Circa ·
· 1760 ·

· Chippendale ·
Style ·

· Measured · & · Drawn · by · Lester Margon

PHILADELPHIA SIDE CHAIR
Detroit Institute of Arts

This Queen Anne side chair in the style of Chippendale, *circa* 1760, is so interesting because it successfully combines the features of several periods. We are fortunate in having the photograph of the accompanying armchair for comparison. The fine features include the carved shell on the top of the back, the eloquent vase-shaped splat, and the refined cabriole legs. They are all blended together by a master cabinetmaker. These chairs are among the best of their kind. This type of chair was made in Philadelphia, Rhode Island, and throughout the Eastern areas. Walnut seems to have been the favored wood but there are also examples in mahogany. Colonial craftsmen favored the Queen Anne style and were loath to abandon it even for the advent of the more sophisticated Chippendale style; therefore they combined the two harmoniously.

QUEEN ANNE SIDE CHAIR
The Henry Francis du Pont Winterthur Museum

This Queen Anne side chair was made in Massachusetts *circa* 1720. A truly beautiful model, it has a shaped seat, cut-out splat, and a carved shell resting at the top, and is true to type in every particular. The splat is elegantly cut in the shape of a vase. Some prefer, however, to call it a fiddle back. The shell carving is repeated on the knee of the cabriole legs, which become quite slender before finishing in ball-and-claw feet. The stretchers are well turned and support the chair amply. It is seldom that one finds so much beauty in a Queen Anne side chair. These chairs continued to be in fashion until the advent of the Chippendale style. However, the American cabinetmakers favored the Queen Anne style and worked in it long after it was supposed to have passed. They used walnut as the preferred wood, especially in New England. These American chairs so surpassed the English prototypes that there is really no comparison. This model is in the Henry Francis du Pont Winterthur Museum.

PAINTED ARMCHAIR

The Henry Francis du Pont Winterthur Museum

This Philadelphia maple armchair is painted black, and was made *circa* 1740-1750. The use of the cyma curves on the splat, seat frame and the legs produces a certain fluid pattern. The chair is a combination of styles, which is ingenious and discloses the master's ability in composition. The old rush seat is supported by the turned stretchers. The various components of the chair identify it as the work of William Savery, whose career continued from 1742 until 1787. The graceful bend of the arms, supported by the excellent turning, is an elegant feature. Somehow this armchair appears to be made up of a collection of heterogenous parts, which is disconcerting. Savery's work ranged from rush seat chairs to Chippendale highboys. While his status as a first rate cabinetmaker is doubtful, much of his work is excellent and is represented in the foremost collections. This armchair may be seen at the Henry Francis du Pont Winterthur Museum.

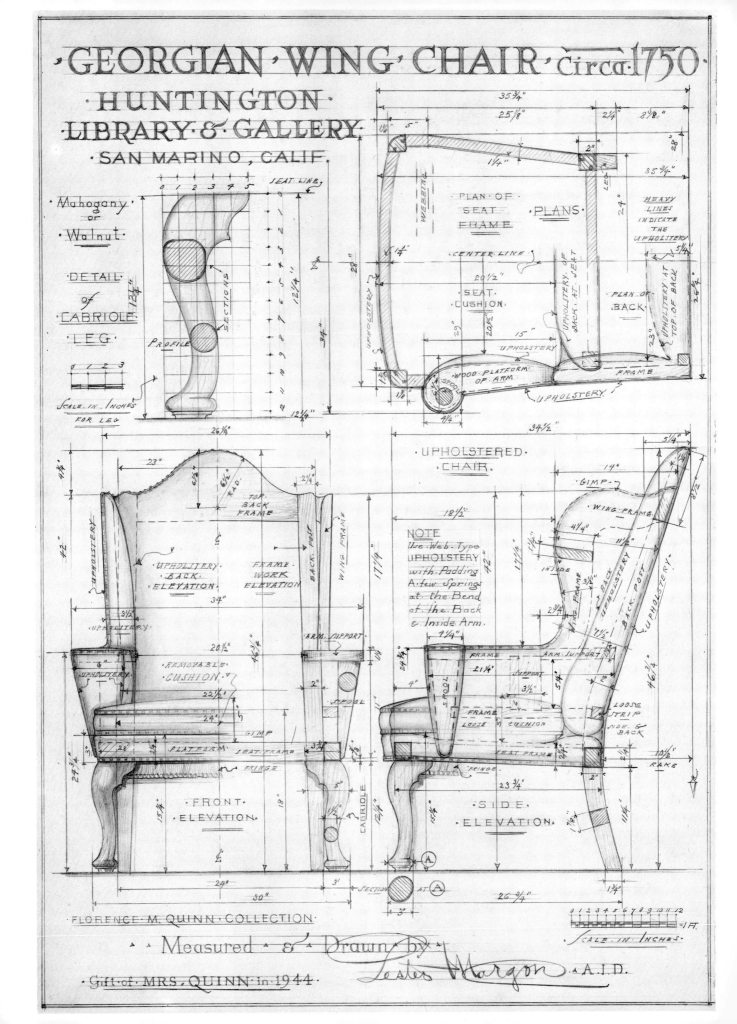

GEORGIAN · WING · CHAIR · Circa · 1750 ·

HUNTINGTON · LIBRARY · & · GALLERY ·
· SAN MARINO, CALIF.

· Mahogany ·
or
· Walnut ·

· DETAIL ·
· of ·
· CABRIOLE ·
· LEG ·

· Scale in Inches ·
FOR LEG

PROFILE — SECTIONS
SEAT LINE

PLAN · OF · SEAT · FRAME
· PLANS ·

WEBBING

CENTER LINE

SEAT · CUSHION

WOOD · PLATFORM · OF · ARM
SPOOL
· UPHOLSTERY ·

PLAN · OF · BACK
FRAME
UPHOLSTERY · AT · TOP · OF · BACK
UPHOLSTERY · OF · BACK · AT · SEAT
HEAVY · LINES · INDICATE · THE · UPHOLSTERY

· UPHOLSTERED · CHAIR ·

NOTE
Use · Web · Type
UPHOLSTERY
with · Padding
A · few · Springs
at · the · Bend
of · the · Back
& · Inside · Arm.

GIMP
WING · FRAME
INSIDE
BACK · UPHOLSTERY
UPHOLSTERY
BACK · POST
ARM · SUPPORT
LOOSE · STRIP
INSIDE · & BACK
RAKE

· TOP · BACK · FRAME ·
RAD.
· UPHOLSTERY · BACK · ELEVATION ·
· FRAME · WORK · ELEVATION ·
BACK · POST
WING · FRAME
ARM · SUPPORT
· REMOVABLE · CUSHION ·
SPOOL
· UPHOLSTERY ·
GIMP
· PLATFORM · SEAT · FRAME ·
FRINGE
· FRONT · ELEVATION ·
CABRIOLE

SPOOL
FRAME
LOOSE · CUSHION
SEAT · FRAME
FRINGE
· SIDE · ELEVATION ·
SUPPORT
LOOSE · CUSHION

SECTION · AT · (A)

· FLORENCE · M · QUINN · COLLECTION ·

· Measured · & · Drawn · by ·

· Gift · of · MRS · QUINN · in · 1944 ·

Lester Margon · A.I.D.

0 1 2 3 4 5 6 7 8 9 10 11 12 = 1 FT.
· SCALE · IN · INCHES ·

GEORGIAN WING CHAIR

Henry E. Huntington Library and Art Gallery   *Mrs. Florence M. Quinn Collection*

This magnificent Georgian Wing Chair is installed in the Upper Maple Drawing Room of the Library of the Henry E. Huntington Library and Art Gallery in San Marino, California. Special permission was granted by the curator to sketch this chair, which was an unheard-of procedure. The lines and the proportions of this chair are superlative and the seating propensities are ingratiating. In fact, this chair attains a perfection that is seldom achieved. The cabriole legs and frame are of walnut. We see many upholstered chairs whose inner construction is a mystery. It is a temptation to look beyond the outer upholstery to see just how the chair was built. There are so many tricks of the trade that must be evoked to produce a finely upholstered chair. Covered in a rare Beau-

vais tapestry, this one is suited to stand in the palace of a king. The graceful lines of the wings, the superb lineation of the spools supporting the arms, and the graceful curve of the top—all contribute to the chair's grandeur. For the visitor to Los Angeles, a visit to the Huntington Library and Art Gallery is a must. And that is not all. Surrounding the buildings is a two hundred acre Botanical Garden with rare and unusual evergreens and deciduous shrubs from many continents. In the Japanese Garden there are many traditional monuments, a moon bridge with weeping willows, a bell-house of the eighteenth century and a period replica of a tea house. Possibly the most unusual feature is the Desert Plants Garden with the largest collection of cacti in the world.

163

THE TAPPAHANNOCK ROOM

The Henry Francis du Pont Winterthur Museum

Dating from 1725, this Tappahannock living room is in the best tradition of the William and Mary period. The settlers brought with them their Continental tastes in furniture and interior design. Of special interest in this setting are the walnut ball-foot chest of drawers dating from 1737 and the interesting mirror above. The desk-on-a-frame is from Pennsylvania. The leather-covered winged armchair is typical of the Moravian settlement in Bethlehem, Pennsylvania. The rather unusual adjustable candlestand is placed next to the caned side chair. Of importance in this room is the caned armchair introducing the "S" and "C" curves in the back. The small side table near this chair supports a spiral set of candles, which may be raised or lowered at will. Altogether this is a very livable room, with the fine panelling, elegant draperies and colorful oriental rug.

CHIPPENDALE WING CHAIR

The Philadelphia Museum of Art

This elaborately carved mahogany upholstered wing chair in the Chippendale style, *circa* 1760, is from Philadelphia, Pennsylvania. It is attributed to Benjamin Randolph of Philadelphia, Pennsylvania. He was established in business on Chestnut Street. His furniture places him as one of the greatest cabinetmakers and carvers of America. This chair, of goodly proportions, is richly carved on arms, legs and apron. The mask in the center of the apron is said to be a portrait of Benjamin Franklin. Be that as it may, the chair was sold at auction for a princely sum. Specimens of his work may be encountered in the Garvin Collection at Yale College, in the Palace at Williamsburg, Virginia, and at the Winterthur Museum. Perhaps there is an overabundance of carving on this wing chair, and the turns may be a little abrupt. However, it is most effective.

CONNECTICUT·SIDE·CHAIR

ART·INSTITUTE·OF·CHICAGO·

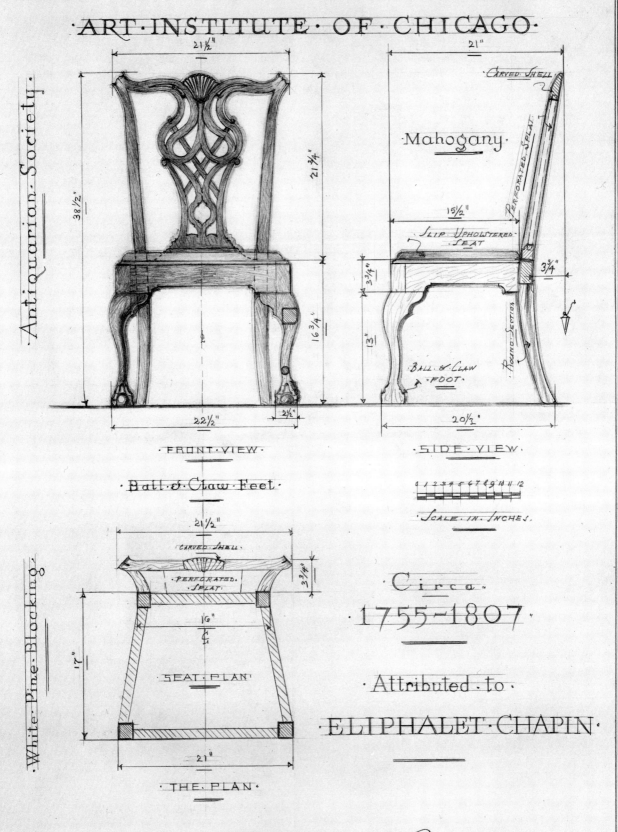

·Antiquarian·Society·

·White·Pine·Blocking·

21½"

21¾"

38½"

16¾"

22½"   2½"

·FRONT·VIEW·

·Ball & Claw Feet·

21"

CARVED SHELL

Mahogany

15½"

SLIP·UPHOLSTERED·SEAT·

3¾"

3¾"

13"

PERFORATED·SPLAT·

ROUND·SECTION·

BALL·&·CLAW·FOOT·

20½"

·SIDE·VIEW·

0 1 2 3 4 5 6 7 8 9 10 11 12

·SCALE·IN·INCHES·

21½"

·CARVED·SHELL·

·PERFORATED·SPLAT·

3¾"

16"

17"

·SEAT·PLAN·

21"

·THE·PLAN·

·Circa·
1755–1807·

·Attributed·to·

·ELIPHALET·CHAPIN·

·Measured·&·Drawn·by·Lester Margon·

CONNECTICUT SIDE CHAIR

The Art Institute of Chicago   Purchase of the Antiquarian Society

This side chair is attributed to Eliphalet Chapin, of East Windsor, *circa* 1755-1805. The Museum notes that "Furniture made in Connecticut during the latter part of the 18th century is distinguished by its construction and imaginative design. The Connecticut craftsmen, somewhat removed from the urban furniture centers such as Boston, Philadelphia and New York, developed an individual style which is particularly appealing. This Connecticut side chair is of the highest quality. The ribboned curves of the center splat extend into the crest to create a smooth plastic quality which contrasts with the stiff cross bars. The graceful but sturdy cabriole legs and the vigorous claw-and-ball feet are in keeping with the character of the chair." This is another example of the virtuosity of the cabinetmakers of this period who created such original and delightful interpretations of the Chippendale style.

167

SHOEMAKER ARMCHAIR
Philadelphia Museum of Art

This very elegant Philadelphia armchair of mahogany was made *circa* 1757-1793 by Jonathan Shoemaker. It is well proportioned and certainly elegantly carved. It was one of a set ordered by a British officer. The back is exquisitely scrolled and the carving is superb. The extended "ears" of the top back rail afford just the proper accents. The repetition of the shell motif at the top and on the front seat rail is unusual. The arms flow in graceful lines to the curved arm supports. The upholstery of the seat is of tapestry of the period. While this armchair entails aspects of the Chippendale style it is distinctly American in conception and design. The cabriole legs are carved at the knees, ending in the usual ball-and-claw feet. The charm of this armchair is undeniable. It has character, distinction and a flair of regality. It is in the collection of the Philadelphia Museum of Art.

CHIPPENDALE STYLE SIDE CHAIR

Metropolitan Museum of Art   Funds from Various Donors, 1951

Certainly incorporating important characteristics of the Chippendale style, this magnificent mahogany side chair is from Philadelphia, *circa* 1760-1775. It is difficult to enumerate all the design elements incorporated in this chair. There are the extended "ears" of the top back rail, and the perforated center back splat of intricate lineation, with the inclusion of carving. The back frame is profusely ornamented with leaf and floral carv-

ings. The cabriole front legs are impressive, ornamented with acanthus leaf carvings at the knee and terminating in the ball-and-claw feet. The chair is in the collection of the American Wing of the Metropolitan Museum of Art and was featured in the 1962 exhibition of "The Anatomy of the Chair." It is certainly one of the handsomest chairs that have been shown in museum collections.

AMERICAN · SIDE · CHAIR

· METROPOLITAN · MUSEUM · OF · ART · N.Y.

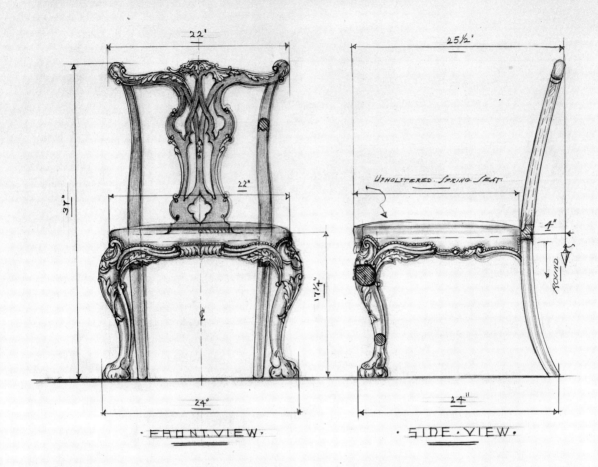

22'

22"

37"

17¼"

24'

· FRONT · VIEW ·

25½"

UPHOLSTERED Spring Seat

4"

ROUND

24"

· SIDE · VIEW ·

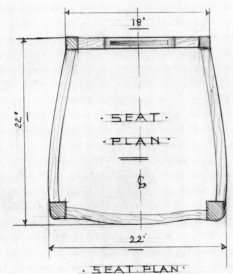

18'

· SEAT · PLAN ·

22'

22'

· SEAT · PLAN ·

· 1 2 3 4 5 6 7 8 9 10 11 12
Scale in Inches

· MAHOGANY ·

· CHIPPENDALE ·
· INFLUENCE ·

· 1760-1780 ·

· Measured · & · Drawn · by · Lester Margon ·

AMERICAN 18TH CENTURY SIDE CHAIR

Metropolitan Museum of Art   Rogers Fund, 1908

This American chair in mahogany, *circa* 1760-1780, shows marked influences of the Chippendale style. Yet, especially from the seat down, there are strong repercussions of the Louis XIV period. The extended scroll "ears" of the top back rail and the complicated pierced interlacing of the back center splat are certainly typical, with a strong Gothic feeling. Chairs of this period were of a great variety and were often unorthodox in treatment. Details of various styles were combined, with little thought given to authenticity. The cabinetmakers seemed to be playing a game to see who could produce the greatest anachronistic product. In this, they succeeded eminently. Of particular interest is the leg of this chair. What a combination of unrelated details that have been fused together in a rather prepossessing manner. It is intriguing, if one does not stress precedent too strongly. The spring upholstered seat is another variance. Despite its apparent irregularities, the chair has a strange majesty that is undeniable. It combines pretense with flamboyance in a remarkable manner.

SIDE CHAIR, STYLE OF CHIPPENDALE

Victoria and Albert Museum, London   *Gift of L. de Renaut, Esq.*

This style of Chippendale side chair in mahogany, *circa* 1760, is in the collection of the Victoria and Albert Museum in London. It incorporates many of the salient characteristics of the work of the master designer and cabinetmaker. It is in the Marlborough grouping, featuring the square leg with the pierced and carved back splat suggestion of Gothic tracery. The extended "ears" of the top rail are typical. Of all the designs illustrated in his book – "Gentleman and Cabinet-maker's Directory," 1754, the chair designs appear to be the most excellent. Chippendale understood chairs and produced them with a virtuosity that was compelling. Others of his chairs featured Chinese motifs, fretwork and elaborate interlacing in the backs. They inclined toward the Rococo but others were Classic in their nature. He was inclined to favor the more fanciful and elaborate designs.

SHIELD-BACK SIDE CHAIR

Metropolitan Museum of Art   The Kennedy Fund, 1918

This Hepplewhite influence shield-back side chair is in mahogany, and dates from *circa* 1785-1795. It is typical of the favored designs of the English designer. It combines grace, charm and elegance. The lines of the shield back flow in harmonious sequence with the top rail of the back in a serpentine curve. The center divisions of the shield are ornamented with husk carvings and towards the top spread out into a fan form. If there is such a thing as perfection, this chair is certainly a candidate for the award. The tapered square front legs with the spade foot are typical. The upholstery is leather. This chair is in the American Wing of the Metropolitan Museum of Art. What a sense of satisfaction is felt upon viewing such perfection. It gives the designer renewed impetus to follow the profession enthusiastically.

173

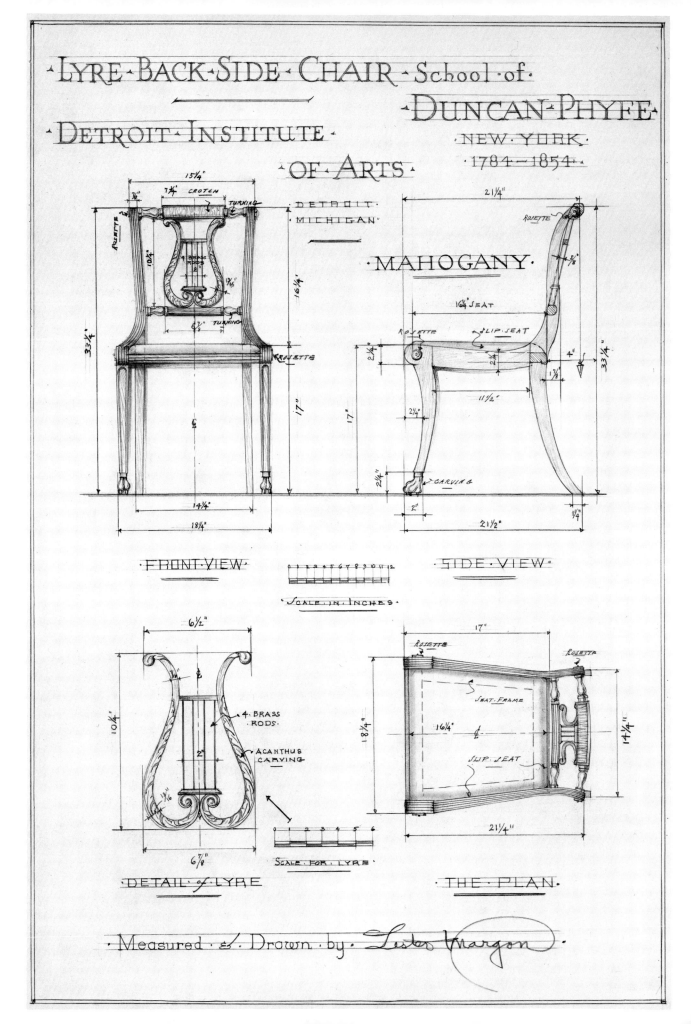

LYRE·BACK·SIDE·CHAIR· School ·of·
DUNCAN·PHYFE·
·DETROIT·INSTITUTE·
NEW·YORK·
·1784—1854·
·OF·ARTS·

·DETROIT·
·MICHIGAN·

MAHOGANY·

·FRONT·VIEW·

·SCALE·IN·INCHES·

·SIDE·VIEW·

·DETAIL· of ·LYRE·

4·BRASS RODS.

ACANTHUS CARVING

·SCALE·FOR·LYRE·

·THE·PLAN·

SEAT·FRAME

SLIP·SEAT

·Measured· & ·Drawn· by· Lester Margon·

LYRE-BACK SIDE CHAIR

The Detroit Institute of Arts

One of the most popular designs in American antique furniture is that of the lyre-back chairs of Duncan Phyfe. The Detroit Institute of Arts is fortunate in having two of these side chairs in its collection. The continuing favor of this type of chair is due to the excellent craftsmanship, the fine sense of design and the deftness in placing carved ornament where it can have a telling effect.

Of course, the lyre form has historical significance and is most pleasing in its appropriateness. The sturdy brass strings almost entice the viewer to play upon them. There is a certain romanticism in this design that is undeniable. The lyre was one of Phyfe's favorite symbols and he used it most often in his furniture designs. Looking at the side view, it presents a vision of Ancient Greece in its purity and fluidity of line. The animal feet are the finishing touch of historical reminiscence. The carving of the acanthus leaves enshrining the framework of the lyre and like a bit of jewelry translated into wood. The lyre form was borrowed from the Directoire mode so popular at the dawn of the 19th century. This influenced the cabinet-makers in America profoundly. If perfection in design is ever realized, this chair is a worthy candidate. There is nothing to find fault with; its euphony deserves only praise and felicitation. While Duncan Phyfe was not an originator or an innovator, he did refine many existing furniture forms. He was a master in handling the carver's tools and his turnings were prolific in their sensibility. No one ever carved an acanthus leaf or rosette with such brilliancy and understanding, as is evident when viewing an example of his craft.

DUNCAN PHYFE SIDE CHAIR

The Cooper-Hewitt Museum of Decorative Arts and Design   *Smithsonian Institution*

This mahogany side chair, New York, *circa* 1815-1830, is in the style of Duncan Phyfe, The lyre was one of the most favored ornaments of Duncan Phyfe, who used it on the backs of chairs and sofas as well as on table bases and on almost everything else that he made. The harp is another matter. It is unique and different and certainly not so popular. Its angular shape does not lend itself to such general use. This side chair is very interesting because of this feature. Aside from its curiosity aspect the chair is graceful and attractive. It might even start a new vogue. The lines are graceful and the details well executed. What a relief to come across a chair that is not stereotyped. In fact, several such chairs in a room might make the atmosphere sing.

WAINSCOT ARMCHAIR

The Henry Francis du Pont Winterthur Museum

Wainscot chairs, popular during the 17th century in America, were fashioned after the wainscoting that was being used in the better houses. They were constructed on straight lines, of oak. These chairs were the seats of honor and generally reserved for the use of the master of the house. They had framed paneled backs, shaped arms, turned legs and straight stretchers. Often, as in this instance, the top rail was ornamented by a piece of added carving. These chairs were of a sturdy type, which may be the reason why many of them have survived to this day. Of course, a loose upholstery cushion was used on the wooden seat. These wainscot chairs have a certain dignity and produce a feeling of the homeliness of these early settlement days. This chair is in the Henry Francis du Pont Winterthur Museum.

The Windsor Chair

The Windsor chair was of English origin, dating from the last quarter of the 17th century. The first chairs of this type were made in Buckinghamshire and were sold for use in farmhouses and taverns. Many were made in a town named Windsor, hence the name. Later these chairs were produced in quantities by rural craftsmen in the neighboring townships such as Suffolk and Yorkshire. The favor of the Windsor chair continued, and it was manufactured in greater quantity than any other type of chair.

The American place of origin of the Windsor chair is not known. The first Windsor chairs were probably made in Philadelphia, *circa* 1725. These early models were adapted from British imported examples but were made to suit the American taste. This consisted of more splay to the legs and a nicety of details. They were so designed as to be better fit for use in the finer residences of a country squire. Many of these chairs featured the comb-back design. The native cabinetmakers developed their own tastes and introduced original characteristics.

This required exceptional skill and fine workmanship. The craftsmen had to be proficient in turning, bending and steaming. The task of shaping a saddle seat was enormous, requiring knowledge and ingenuity. The carved volutes at the ends of the top rails had to be proficiently executed. A diversity of woods were used in the making of these chairs, including pine, maple, white-wood, chestnut, hickory and ash. After the chairs were completed many were painted to the desires of the purchasers.

There were so many kinds of Windsor chairs that only a few may be mentioned. They included the low-back, the comb-back, the fan-back, the hoop-back and many others. Many connoisseurs consider the comb-back the noblest of them all.

The writing Windsor chair is believed to have originated in America. There was an extended right arm which served as a writing surface. Below this arm was a small drawer to hold writing materials. Below the seat was a larger drawer which held stationery and leaflets used by the occupant. There were only a few left-handed Windsor chairs made. The backs were high so that the writer could rest his head.

It is an historical fact that Thomas Jefferson was seated in a writing Windsor chair when he first composed the draft for the Declaration of Independence in June of 1776. The original chair is now in the collection of the American Philadelphia Society. It is known that at the time of the death of George Washington in 1799, there were more than thirty Windsor chairs on the portico at Mt. Vernon.

The Windsor settee, in various shapes and sizes, developed later, *circa* 1750. It was made to seat from two to five persons. The front of the seat was straight with a slight suggestion of saddling. The back was low with a continuous arm and an applied cresting held in place by numerous plain spindles. The settees had many legs and required recessed stretchers of bulbous turnings and well splayed legs.

The well-known firm of John K. Cowperthwaite, 1815-1835, then located at No. 4 Chatham Square in New York City, had a large assortment of Windsor chairs and painted fancy chairs of the latest and most elegant variety. In fact, at this time Windsor chairs were featured in the best furniture emporiums.

The "Boston Rocker" was a development of the Windsor rocker, 1820-1855. These were painted and decorated with stencils of fruit and flowers, also landscapes with much striping. Many of them are imposing and certainly homelike. They graced many parlors in the finest residences of the time.

There are few articles that are essentially American. The Windsor chair and the Boston rocker are two of which we may be rightfully proud.

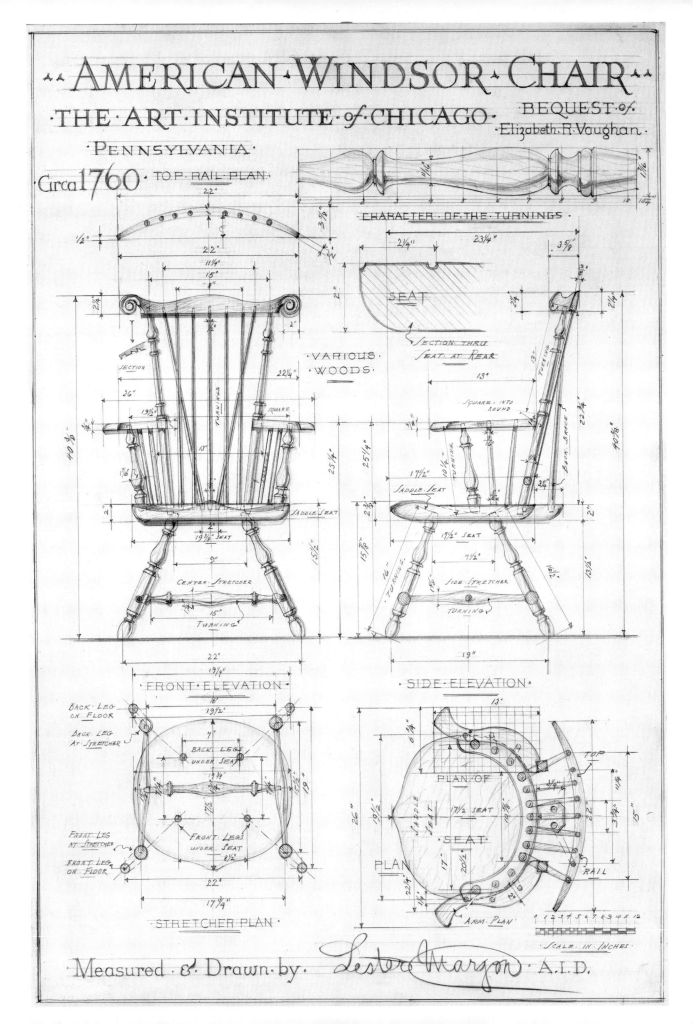

AMERICAN · WINDSOR · CHAIR

THE · ART · INSTITUTE · of · CHICAGO ·

BEQUEST · of ·
Elizabeth · R · Vaughan ·

· PENNSYLVANIA ·
Circa 1760 · TOP · RAIL · PLAN ·

· CHARACTER · OF · THE · TURNINGS ·

· SEAT ·
SECTION · THRU ·
SEAT · AT · REAR ·

· VARIOUS ·
· WOODS ·

SQUARE · INTO ·
ROUND ·

SECTION

TURNINGS

SQUARE

SADDLE · SEAT

SADDLE · SEAT

CENTER · STRETCHER

TURNING

SIDE · STRETCHER

TURNING

· FRONT · ELEVATION ·

· SIDE · ELEVATION ·

BACK · LEG
ON · FLOOR

BACK · LEG
AT · STRETCHER

BACK · LEGS
UNDER · SEAT

PLAN · OF

TOP

FRONT · LEGS
UNDER · SEAT

PLAN

SADDLE
SEAT

SEAT

FRONT · LEG
AT · STRETCHER

RAIL

FRONT · LEG
ON · FLOOR

· STRETCHER · PLAN ·

ARM · PLAN ·

· SCALE · IN · INCHES ·

Measured · & · Drawn · by · Lester Margon · A.I.D.

FAN-BACK WINDSOR CHAIR

The Art Institute of Chicago   *Bequest of Elizabeth R. Vaughan*

The Art Institute of Chicago is the center of the cultural life of the Mid-west. So varied and manifold are its collections that the section of American furniture is only one of the many divisions of the decorative arts. This fan-back Windsor chair is one of the finest models that have come to our attention. It is from Pennsylvania, *circa* 1750-1780. As usual many woods were incorporated in the making of this chair. The top rail is deeply concave and at the ends are carved volutes. The rail decreases in weight almost to a knife-edge at the top. The back and arm supports are turned in the "tulip" style. The legs are decidedly raked, with the top entering the seat about 4″ from the perimeter. The legs are held in place by plain turnings. It requires a single block of wood about 2½″ thick to form the saddle seat which is shaped and gouged out until the proper seating comfort has been obtained. At the center of the seat the wood is brought to a pointed swelling. A groove is cut towards the back of the seat surrounding the spindles. The graceful arms conform with the plan of the top rail. American Windsor chairs were delicately fashioned and knowingly designed, with turnings that had grace and eloquence. They are far superior to Windsor chairs fabricated in England. There are many types of Windsor chairs including hoop, fan, comb and low backs. The fan-back type is considered the finest.

LOOP-BACK WINDSOR CHAIR

The Art Institute of Chicago   Gift of Mrs. Emily Crane Chadbourne

Possibly the simplest type of Windsor chair is the loop-back model where a continuous bend serves as the arm and the back frame of the chair. It requires considerable skill to form this type of chair because there are no back supports, only shaped turned spindles going from the seat directly into the bend of the back. This model came from Fishkill, New York, *circa* 1775. The turnings of the legs, arm supports and the stretchers are excellent. The saddle seat is conservatively shaped, not too deeply cut but sufficient for seating comfort. The broad leg base affords the necessary aplomb for the chair. There are fancier and more complicated designs of Windsor chairs but none more satisfactory. This model is in the collection of the Art Institute of Chicago.

THE WINDSOR SETTEE

The Henry Francis du Pont Winterthur Museum

When a design becomes popular it is often developed into many forms. This was true in the case of the Windsor settee, *circa* 1750-1770. The size varied from the love seat to one accommodating four or more persons. The front of the seat was always straight with little saddling. The back was divided into divisions as may be required, supported by structural bends, according to the length of the settee. The arm was continuous, intercepted by the required number of turned spindles. The legs were well splayed, with bulbous turnings. Many of these settees were used in dormitories and institutions as they were not particularly attractive in home living rooms. There were no special structural difficulties to be encountered except that it was difficult to secure the required length of boards for the seats. Because of this fact, the saddling was never too deep or varied in curvatures.

COMB~BACK · WINDSOR · CHAIR ·

FINE · ARTS · GALLERY · OF · SAN · DIEGO ·

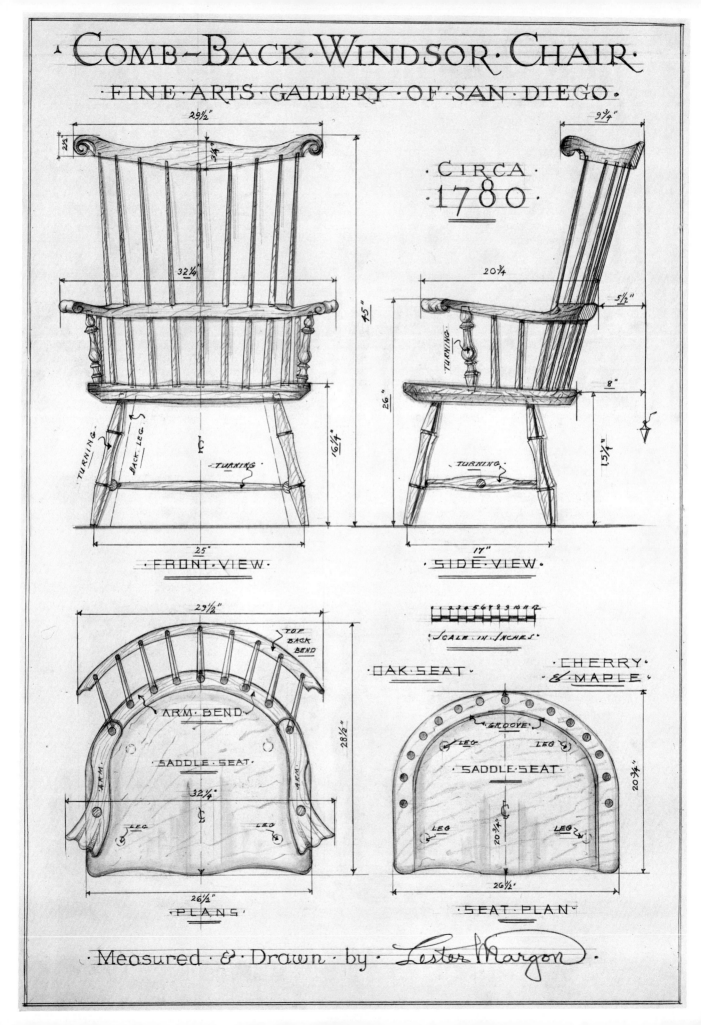

CIRCA 1780

· FRONT · VIEW ·

· SIDE · VIEW ·

TOP BACK BEND

ARM · BEND ·

SADDLE · SEAT ·

· PLANS ·

SCALE · IN · INCHES ·

· OAK · SEAT ·

· CHERRY · & · MAPLE ·

GROOVE

LEG   LEG

SADDLE · SEAT ·

LEG   LEG

· SEAT · PLAN ·

· Measured · & · Drawn · by · Lester Margon ·

COMB-BACK WINDSOR CHAIR

The Fine Arts Gallery, San Diego   The Gift of Miss Elsie Kimberly

This high-back Windsor armchair is distinctive by reason of its stability. It was made in Massachusetts, *circa* 1780. The saddle seat is carved from a solid 2″ block of oak. It is finely shaped for seating comfort. Other parts of the chair were made of cherry and maple. The substantial arm which continues as the back support is so fashioned that the spindles pass through it uninterrupted. The bent top rail ends in carved volutes. The hand-hold of the arm is finely carved and spreads out invitingly. There are nine back spindles which is the greatest number to be found in this type of chair. Many Windsor chairs were later painted to the inclinations of the purchasers

although the wood finish seems more appropriate. More than any other type of chair, the Windsor has continued to hold favor. During the second half of the 18th century these chairs were made in great quantities in factories located all through the Colonies. The making of the Windsor chair required great skill of design and expert workmanship. The bows, the continuous bends and the fine turnings were not a simple performance. The comb-back type was perhaps the most complicated and the most expensive. It was widely sought after. This model is in the collection of the Fine Arts Gallery of San Diego, Balboa Park, California.

THE HARVEST ROOM

Shelburne Museum, Shelburne, Vermont

Photo by Taylor and Dull, New York (Courtesy of Antiques *Magazine)*

One of the most typical rooms in the Shelburne Museum, Shelburne, Vermont, is the Harvest Room of the Dutton House from Cavendish, Vermont. The house was inhabited by the Dutton and Proctor families for several generations. In the photograph the center of interest is the book-keeper's desk mounted on the trestle base with the accompanying high stool. Also shown are splendid examples of a rod-back Windsor chair and a New England comb-back model. The hanging corner-cabinet, the two long open shelves above the desk, the game table, the samovar and the two bristling spittoons all show that this was a room to be lived in. Note the stencils on the walls and the suggestion of a dentil cornice. The high lift-top desk is an unique 18th century New England piece, on a trestle sawbuck base.

COMB-BACK WINDSOR CHAIR

Art Institute of Chicago   Gift of Mrs. Emily Crane Chadbourne

This superb model of a comb-back Windsor chair is from Pennsylvania, *circa* 1750. The proportions are excellent. The carved "ears" terminate in a scroll, and the continuous arm rail is intercepted by a series of turned spindles. The saddle seat is well shaped for comfort. The tulip turnings are excellent in the legs, arm supports and the turned stretchers. The wide rake of the legs affords an excellent balance for this chair. While Philadelphia was the original center for the manufacturing of Windsor chairs, soon factories were set up in surrounding cities. The American Windsor chair is so superior to the English prototype that it may well be called an American invention. This chair is in the collection of the Art Institute of Chicago.

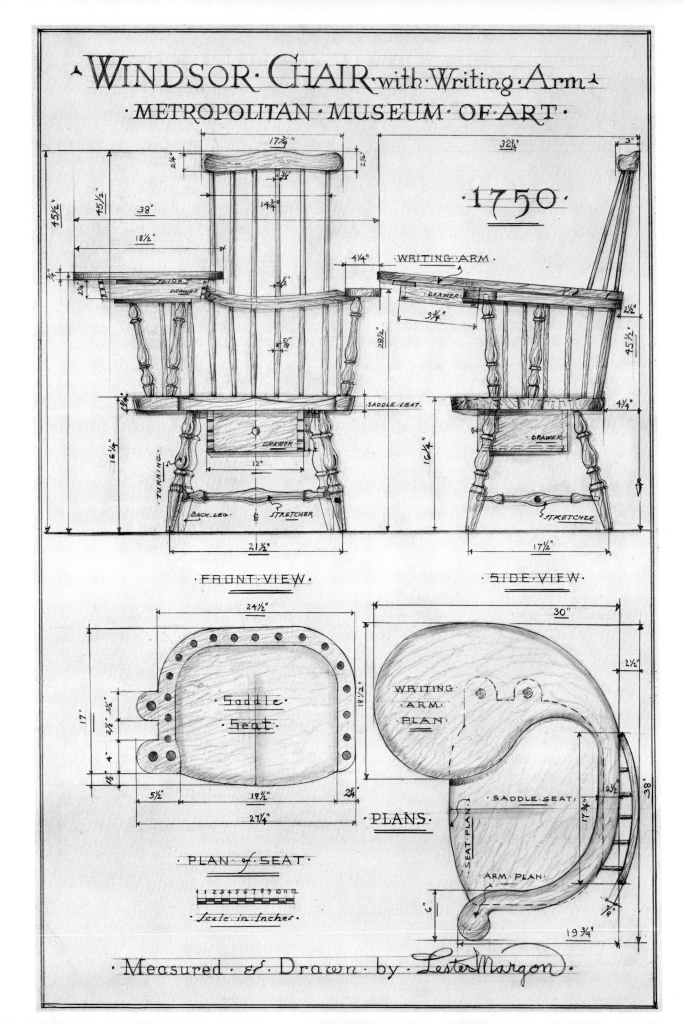

WINDSOR·CHAIR·with·Writing·Arm·
·METROPOLITAN·MUSEUM·OF·ART·

·1750·

WRITING·ARM

SADDLE·SEAT

DRAWER

DRAWER

SLIDE

TURNING

BACK·LEG

STRETCHER

STRETCHER

·FRONT·VIEW·

·SIDE·VIEW·

·Saddle·
·Seat·

WRITING
ARM
PLAN

SADDLE·SEAT

SEAT·PLAN

ARM·PLAN

·PLANS·

·PLAN·of·SEAT·

1 2 3 4 5 6 7 8 9 10 11 12

·Scale·in·Inches·

·Measured·&·Drawn·by·Lester Margon·

WINDSOR CHAIR WITH WRITING ARM

Metropolitan Museum of Art   Gift of Mrs. Screven Lorillard, 1952

This type of Windsor chair with a writing arm is one of the few American originals in furniture design. While the first Windsors in this country were probably made in the vicinity of Philadelphia, *circa* 1725, this model from New England dates from the middle of the 18th century. The extensive writing surface of the extended right arm has a small drawer beneath, fitted with a slide that may be pulled out to hold a candle so the occupant may see better what he is doing. Below is a small drawer to hold writing materials. Below the shaped seat is a larger drawer for leaflets or books. Wallace Nutting called this kind of chair "A world within itself." Emerson is said to have written many of his essays seated in such a chair. It is known that Thomas Jefferson was seated in his Windsor chair when he wrote the first drafts of the Declaration of Independence. So, these chairs have many historical associations. Various types of wood were used in the making of Windsor chairs including hickory, maple and oak. Note that the arm is continuous and is pierced by a series of spindles held in place at the top by a curved comb-back top rail. A more detailed study of Windsor chairs is found on page 178. It is a most interesting subject.

KITCHEN OF THE VERMONT HOUSE

The Shelburne Museum, Shelburne, Vermont

Photo by Taylor & Dull, New York (Courtesy of Antiques *Magazine)*

Although the kitchen of the Vermont House has been completely redecorated, much of the original setting remains as shown. The room is particularly interesting because of the furniture as well as the household objects, colorful pottery and gleaming pewter. The ball-foot chest of drawers is decorated in black and red on a dull orange ground. The candlesticks on top are of turned slate. Especially noteworthy is the purple Delft tile depicting a cat and dog barnyard scene. The center table with pad feet stands on a colorful rag rug. Very amusing and most unusual is the mellowed gray Windsor chair in the corner with its bowed and spindled superstructure. Facing the table is a fan-back Windsor chair. The ever-ready spinning wheel waits nearby and the wooden candle stand may be raised or lowered. In Colonial America the kitchen was the center of the family's activities, where they gathered at meal times and discussed the news of the day, heightened by the little bits of gossip collected.

INFANT'S WINDSOR HIGH CHAIR

The Brooklyn Museum, New York

This Windsor style infant's high chair was made of walnut, *circa* 1750, in Philadelphia. Although it originated in England, it was in America that the Windsor chair developed into various types and was used generally. This bow-back high chair is especially interesting because of its ingratiating size and silhouette. The step, for the child to rest its feet on, is well placed. The wide splay of the legs prevents the chair from tipping. Beyond its practicality, this chair is beautiful in line and demeanor. Any infant should be happy to use it. It is remarkable how well the basic Windsor form lends itself to so many variations and uses. There is a certain universality about it that is compelling.

191

HITCHCOCK · ROCKING · CHAIR ·

The · BROOKLYN · MUSEUM ·

NEW · YORK ·

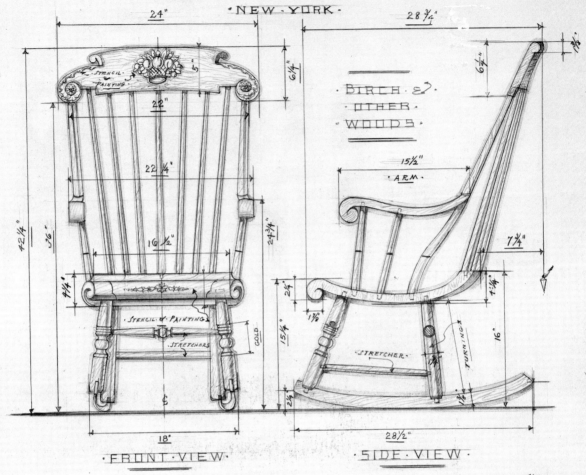

· BIRCH · & · OTHER · WOODS ·

FRONT · VIEW ·

SIDE · VIEW ·

· AMERICAN ·

· Early ·

· 19th · Century ·

· Riverton ~ Conn · ·

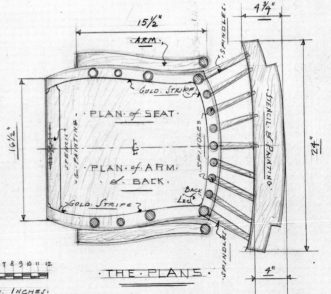

PLAN of SEAT

PLAN of ARM & BACK

· THE · PLANS ·

0 1 2 3 4 5 6 7 8 9 10 11 12
· SCALE · IN · INCHES ·

· Measured · & · Drawn · by · Lester Margon ·

HITCHCOCK ROCKER
Brooklyn Museum

There are few pieces of furniture that are so typically American as the Boston rocker. On this model appears the mark as follows – "Hitchcock, Alford & Co. Hitchcocksville, Connecticut/Warranted – *Circa* 1832." The rocking chair is of goodly proportions with a high back of seven spindles, held in place by a shaped crest rail. The chair is painted black and decorated with a light brown flower basket design on the crest and a floral spray on the edge of the seat. There is an abundance of striping. The seat is especially impressive and difficult to manufacture. The seat of

pine is upturned at the rear and boldly rolled at the front. These are separate pieces of wood fastened to the otherwise flat seat. This type of seat is known as "a rolling seat." It is very comfortable. These rockers were to be found in all types of homes and graced many a porch of the better houses. Another feature is the cyma curved arms ending at the handhold in a scroll. The leg turnings are typical and touched off in gold. The simple turned stretchers hold the base together. What a pleasure it is to come across a Boston Rocker in the countryside. They are indeed homelike.

SPINDLE-BACK ROCKER
Shaker Museum, Old Chatham

This spindle-back rocker is from Mt. Lebanon, New York, *circa* 1880. It is one of the major types illustrated in their catalogues. It is a distinct design with shaped spindles in the back held together by a lower and top rail. The front and back posts are turned. The woven rush seat is typical. The quaint little stool is well constructed. The rocker is inviting and comfortable; that is, if rockers are favored. It was at Mt. Lebanon that the Shakers set up their largest and most significant colony. It is important to note that women were the dominant and creative personalities in the Shaker Movement. The two reasons were theological and psychological. Inspired by their leader, Mother Ann Lee, according to their covenant, procreation was sin. This of course, was the reason for the demise of the movement as well as lack of popular support of their industries.

SHAKER ROCKER

The Cooper-Hewitt Museum of Decorative Arts and Design, Smithsonian Institution
The Gift of Mrs. Jacob M. Kaplan

In considering Shaker furniture it is necessary not alone to appreciate the technicalities of the design, but also to understand the principles which motivated their work. The Shakers evolved a furniture style that blended purity with the doctrines of the celibate life. This furniture combines a restraint in design, a striving for perfection in craftsmanship and above all the utilitarian objective. They had a passion for simplicity and a striving for excellence in execution. This slat-back rocker exemplifies these ideals. It is spacious, comfortable and attractive. The rush seat is held securely between the front and rear posts. The little strip at the top is unusual, probably to serve as a head rest. The rocker is marked "Shaker's / Trade mark / Mt. Lebanon, New York." It is made of stained cherry or maple, *circa* 1890. A visit to the Shaker Museum at Old Chatham, New York, is a thrilling experience. There can be seen the living quarters and the workshops of the former community.

LIST OF ILLUSTRATIONS

(Asterisks indicate photographs accompanied by measured drawings.)

THE LURE
OF THE ANTIQUE

5

At a recent auction sale in a well-known gallery on Madison Avenue in New York, an antique walnut dresser, a beautiful example of Pennsylvania German cabinetmaking was knocked down for $16,000.

* * *

On April 27, 1927 at the Reifsnyder sale, a celebrated highboy was sold for $44,000. This Philadelphia highboy brought the highest price ever paid for a single piece of furniture at auction.

* * *

A mahogany tea table brought the price of $29,000 at auction. It is by John I. Goddard from the collection of Philip Flayderman of Boston. The sale was held at the American Art Association.

* * *

EVERY season at public auctions many thousands of dollars worth of antique furniture is put up for sale. This fact makes one wonder about the reason for this continued interest. What is the state of mind of the purchasers who are willing and anxious to part with large sums of money to possess these pieces of old furniture?

Certainly, the intrinsic value of many of these antiques is dubious. Their real worth cannot be readily ascertained. There is no lexicon to consult and no price list to guide us. It is all so subtle and intangible. However, the amount of buying and selling at these auction rooms is tremendous. Why is it that America is the happy selling ground for antiques from all corners of the globe?

Generally, the pieces of furniture and objets d'art are put on exhibition several days prior to the sale. Individuals, collectors, dealers and museum representatives view the pieces that are to be offered for sale. In catalogues, often costing from $1 to $10, a brief summary of each article is listed, giving very little information as to the real value and identity of the pieces. One must depend largely on the integrity of the galleries sponsoring the sale. The gullible public accepts this without question. In rare instances where misrepresentation has been alleged, the cases have been settled quietly out of court.

Although most auction sales are legitimate, it is our contention that buyers are entitled to greater protection. Along with each piece of furniture listed in the catalogue should appear a clear photograph and detailed description giving dates and data. Of course, dealers and museum personnel can readily determine the status and value of antiques. The uninformed buyer will do well to consult an appraiser before going too deeply into bidding for antiques.

At the appointed hour the sale begins. The hall is crowded. People are standing at the rear. As each piece of furniture is placed on the platform a wave of excitement passes through the audience. By clever speech and manipulation, the auctioneer, assisted by his cohorts scattered throughout the assemblage, creates a state of hysteria. In the excitement of the moment, buyers compete with one another, often raising the price of the objects far beyond their real worth.

All informed purchasers realize that the supply of genuine antiques is continually diminishing. There is no source for replacements. Year after year, by bequests, purchases and acquisitions, the finest antiques are being added to museum collections. Here they are restored when needed and taken good care of. These antiques are installed for the viewing, study and enjoyment of students, collectors, antiquarians, designers and furniture manufacturers, as well as the general public. When a known rare antique does come up for sale, the price often increases to such astronomical figures that only the affluent can compete for its purchase.

All furniture that is old and needs not necessarily be good. Age is not the criterion in determining the quality or the value of antiques.

Only the archeologist places time before all else. By an Act of Congress, only foreign antiques made before January 1st, 1830 are admitted into this country free of duty. This is a purely arbitrary regulation. Time has a way of scrapping the unworthy in the survival of the fittest. For a piece of furniture to remain intact for a hundred years or more proves that it it was well made and has received more than ordinary care.

For family or sentimental reasons, pieces of furniture have been handed down from one generation to another. In the 17th century, it was customary for parents to give their children a generous portion of their household goods at the time of their marriage. This was often stipulated in wills noting to whom the particular pieces of furniture were bequeathed. In 1368, Lord Ferris left his son, "My green bed with arms thereon." The will of William Shakespeare provided for "The interlineated bequest to his wife, the second best bed." The best bed would remain in the principal guest chamber.

However, there are far more important reasons why antique furniture should be revered. The first and foremost justification should be that it is an "original." Then it should be the work of a recognized designer or cabinet-maker. It should be distinct, unique and different from all that has gone before. It should express the taste and the milieu of the particular period. Couple with this historical associations. For instance, the desk used by George Washington, now resting quietly in the Governor's Room in the New York City Hall, has greater value because of its historical association. The table on which the Treaty of Versailles was signed in the Hall of Mirrors is another noteworthy example. But a genuine Sheraton or Chippendale chair may be worth its weight in gold by reason of its fine proportions and excellent design and workmanship.

Besides sentiment, design and historical associations, antique furniture has a far greater significance. It reflects the time and political strategy of each succeeding decade. The study of antique furniture is the sesame that unlocks the storehouse of legend, romance and tradition. From the gay cavorting of the Court of Louis XV to the staunch restrictions set by the Pilgrim Fathers, this antique furniture remains the articulate evidence of "Once Upon a Time." Records that history has failed to relate live again in these pieces of antique furniture. It has been said that the history of furniture is the history of civilization. Perhaps that is why so many people today seek this much-needed background in an attempt to associate themselves with the august past, in the perilous present. In doing so, they become a part of the rich historical backdrop and receive its revelation.

Anyone who is interested in antique furniture should frequent the museums and study the pieces on exhibition. Learn the dates, history and the salient characteristics of each period. Public libraries have a wealth of material on the subject. Home magazines and Sunday pictorials are a splendid source of information. One can hardly take up a daily newspaper without finding some article on furniture and decoration.

Model rooms in new apartment complexes and suburban developments offer opportunities to see the finest ensembles created by the foremost interior designers. These decorators have a flair for combining antiques with exemplary contemporary furniture. Of course, few of us can afford to have antiques in the home. However, there are truly splendid reproductions being made by reputable furniture manufacturers. These can be purchased at reasonable prices and will stand up so much better in everyday use.

"The Lure of the Antique" is one of those unreasonable obsessions that many people enjoy. It sends a lightning shock into an otherwise placid existence. This study and appreciation of the glories of the past defeats the apathy of present day conformity. It makes the mirage of the "Good Old Days" appear valid, helping to ease the maelstrom of chaotic conditions in which we find ourselves today.

The story from the times of the first settlers in Jamestown to the regal events of the Federal period is an expanse so rich that it can afford endless pleasure and satisfaction in research and understanding. One can become akin to the drama and the development of our great country. It is an exciting and rewarding journey that will never lead you astray.

CLASSICAL·REVIVAL·SIDEBOARD

DETROIT·INSTITUTE·OF·ARTS

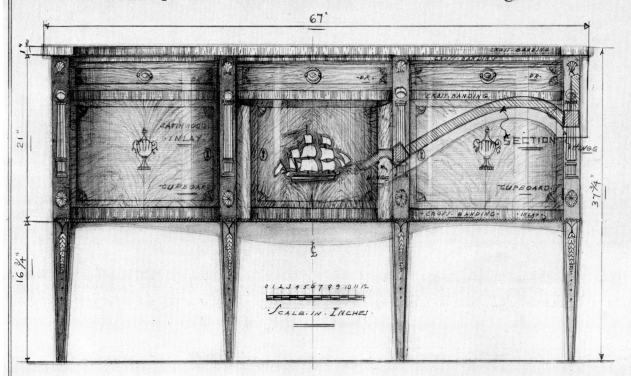

67"

21"

16 ¾"

37 ¾"

CROSS BANDING

SATINWOOD INLAY

CROSS BANDING

DR.

CROSS BANDING

DR.

SECTION

HINGE

CUPBOARD

HINGE

CUPBOARD

CROSS BANDING INLAY

0 1 2 3 4 5 6 7 8 9 10 11 12
SCALE IN INCHES

·FRONT·VIEW·

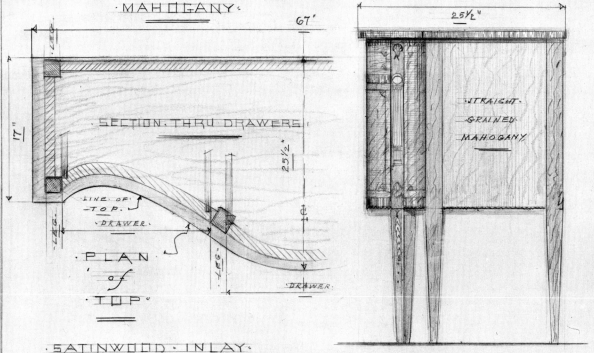

·FLAMBOYANT·
·MAHOGANY·

67"

17"

·SECTION·THRU·DRAWERS·

25½"

·LINE·OF·
·TOP·
·DRAWER·

18"

·LEG·

·LEG·

·LEG·

·DRAWER·

·PLAN·
·of·
·TOP·

·SATINWOOD·INLAY·

25½"

·STRAIGHT·
·GRAINED·
·MAHOGANY·

·SIDE·VIEW·

·Measured·&·Drawn·by· Lester Margon

CLASSICAL REVIVAL SIDEBOARD

Detroit Institute of Arts   Gift of Miss Grace Tower in memory of Miss Nell Tower

This Hepplewhite sideboard of mahogany, *circa* 1780-1800, was probably made in Baltimore, Maryland. The Classical revival was a period that knew no bounds. The exaltation of the New Republic found expression in all forms of design. In this sideboard the serpentine plan is exaggerated, the mahogany is flamboyant and the crotch matched. Borders are cross-banded and the satinwood inlay is freely taken from Greek ornament, going so far as to include an architectural column in the leg posts. Of course, the most striking innovation in this sideboard is the inclusion of the center inlay depicting a sailing vessel. No doubt this piece was made to order for a sea captain who was intent upon having a picture of his worthy craft ever present. Despite the magnifications, this sideboard is prepossessing. The space division is perfect and the placing of the inlay compelling. Call it a *tour de force* if you will, but this sideboard is mightily exciting and incomprehensible. What a joy to come across a piece that is a phenomenon.

LATE 18TH CENTURY SIDEBOARD

Metropolitan Museum of Art   Gift of Mitchell Taradash and the Pulitzer Fund, 1945

The mahogany sideboard with inlays of boxwood, ebony and satinwood, dates from the late 18th century. On the top is a knife box with tambour front and two lower drawers. The shaped front of the sideboard consists of four drawers under the top and a series of cabinets below. There are eight tapered legs edged with inlay and fitted with brass casters on a wheeled base. This great mass is broken by the use of contrasted woods and the accents of inlay, as well as the heraldic painting on the central arched panel. It is indeed a virtuoso performance so popular in the Federal period. This sideboard is an American interpretation of the English Regency which was known as the age of elegance. There was no limit to the elaboration of the furniture being created. The country was exuberant in its ecstacy of the New Republic and knew no limits to its glorification. The sideboard is in the American Wing of the Metropolitan Museum of Art.

MAHOGANY SIDEBOARD

The Wadsworth Atheneum, Hartford, Connecticut   *Bequest of Frederick A. Robbins, Jr.*

This Hepplewhite mahogany sideboard, *circa* 1804, was made by Aaron Chapin in Hartford, Connecticut. He was the second cousin of the famous cabinetmaker Eliphalet Chapin in whose shop Aaron learned his trade. Aaron was socially inclined, and intimated that any clients who would favor him with their patronage would be assured of "fidelity and dispatch." He made a selection of cherry and mahogany house furniture. This side-board is one of his best products. The intricate serpentine plan, the splendid selection of the crotch with just enough inlay make it a most attractive piece. There are various sized drawers at the top with cupboards below. The variations of size and the determining of the plan are quite complicated. The piece has eight legs which are square, tapered and inlaid. Altogether this side-board is one of the finest.

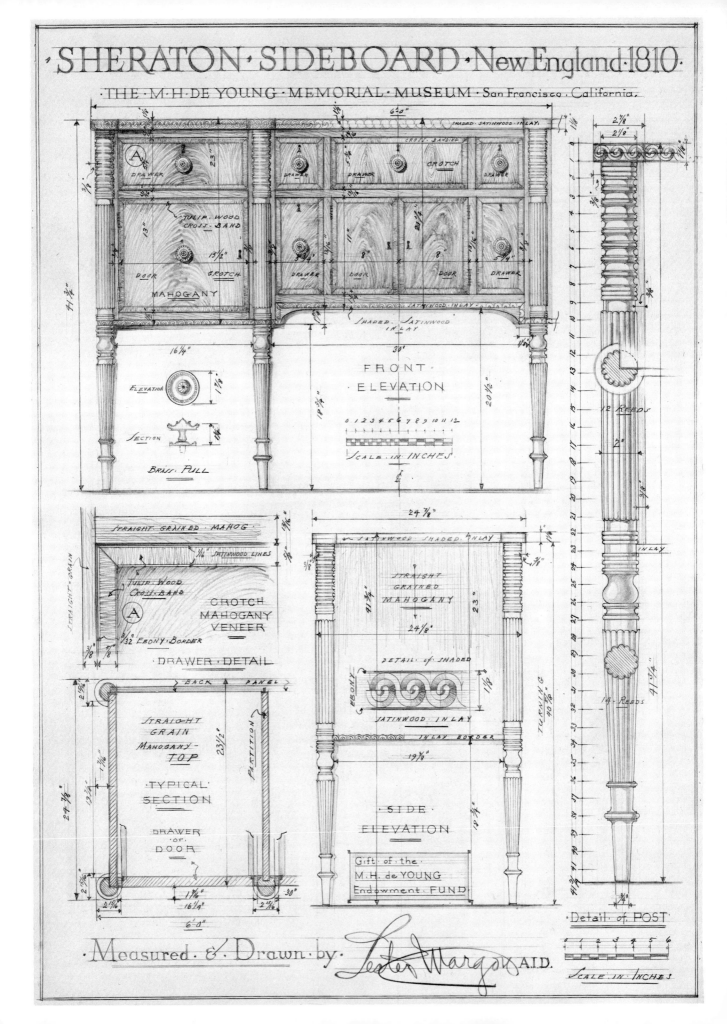

SHERATON · SIDEBOARD · New England · 1810 ·

THE · M·H·DE YOUNG · MEMORIAL · MUSEUM · San Francisco · California ·

FRONT · ELEVATION

SCALE · IN · INCHES

0 1 2 3 4 5 6 7 8 9 10 11 12

BRASS · PULL

ELEVATION

SECTION

DRAWER

DOOR

CROTCH

MAHOGANY

TULIP · WOOD CROSS · BAND

SHADED · SATINWOOD · INLAY

CROSS · BANDING

CROTCH

SHADED · SATINWOOD INLAY

SATINWOOD · INLAY

STRAIGHT · GRAINED · MAHOG

1/16" SATINWOOD LINES

TULIP WOOD CROSS · BAND

CROTCH MAHOGANY VENEER

1/32 EBONY · BORDER

DRAWER · DETAIL

STRAIGHT GRAIN MAHOGANY · TOP

TYPICAL SECTION

DRAWER OR DOOR

BACK PANEL

PARTITION

SATINWOOD SHADED · INLAY

STRAIGHT GRAINED MAHOGANY

DETAIL · of SHADED

EBONY

SATINWOOD · INLAY

INLAY · BORDER

SIDE · ELEVATION

Gift · of · the · M·H· de YOUNG Endowment · FUND

12 REEDS

14 REEDS

INLAY

TURNING 40 7/8"

41 3/4"

· Detail · of · POST

SCALE · IN · INCHES

0 1 2 3 4 5 6

· Measured · & · Drawn · by · Lester Margon A.I.D.

SHERATON SIDEBOARD

M. H. de Young Memorial Museum   Gift of M. H. de Young Endowment Fund

This magnificent sideboard in mahogany with holly and satinwood is in the Sheraton style from New England, *circa* 1810. It is one of the most prepossessing pieces in the collection of furniture in the M. H. de Young Memorial Museum in Golden Gate Park in San Francisco. There are so many interesting details in this sideboard that it will be well to point out just a few. Particularly attractive are the superimposed turned legs with horizontal reeding near the top and vertical reeding in the lower portions. This gives the sideboard an unusual structural importance. The minute scroll detail of the inlay at the top front edge and the inlay at the bottom of the case are remarkable in delineation. What makes this sideboard so

spectacular is the selection and the arrangement of the crotch mahogany veneers on the front. The flamelike brilliancy is compelling. The fine raised knobs give just the right accents to the front elevation. There are drawers and cupboards of various sizes. The excellent photograph is worthy of close scrutiny. It gives an unusually fine impression of the excellent space divisions. This sideboard is certainly a bravura performance in cabinet-work. The interiors of the upper drawers are divided for the placement of cutlery. The cupboards are for storage. What a splendid combination of Colonial design coupled with the influence of the work of Thomas Sheraton in a Federal interpretation.

FEDERAL MIRROR

The Henry Francis du Pont Winterthur Museum

This mahogany and gilt Federal mirror is the closest interpretation of the Robert Adam style made in America. This mirror was made in New York or possibly in Connecticut, *circa* 1790-1800. It was formerly in the Sylmaris Collection, a gift of George Coe Graves, 1931. The voluminous scroll work and especially the detail of the head-piece are certainly prolific. The central cup-like carved parts serve well as starting points for the succeeding scrolls, variations and cups. This affords a proper vantage point for the succeeding scrolls. This detail is carried down on the sides and is repeated at the base. Certainly this looking glass is a masterful expression of the dilatory exuberance of the Adam style and fits well into the extravaganza of the Federal Period. This example is in the Henry Francis du Pont Winterthur Museum.

SHERATON SIDEBOARD

Art Institute of Chicago   Gift of the Antiquarian Society   The Mrs. Clive Runnells Fund

This mahogany and inlaid sideboard is attributed to Mathew Egerton, New Jersey, *circa* 1790. The serpentine front is divided into three sections, the two ends being cupboards as well as the central set-back section. There are four drawers of equal size above. This piece shows the high standard of work produced by the American cabinetmakers at this time. One gets the sense that the heavy bulk is actually floating in the air, although in actuality, it is supported by six tapered legs. The mahogany crotch is flamboyant, contrasted by the inlays of satinwood and the cross-banded borders. This is truly a masterpiece, one of the most elaborate of its kind. It might be classified as Sheraton although it contains many American attributes.

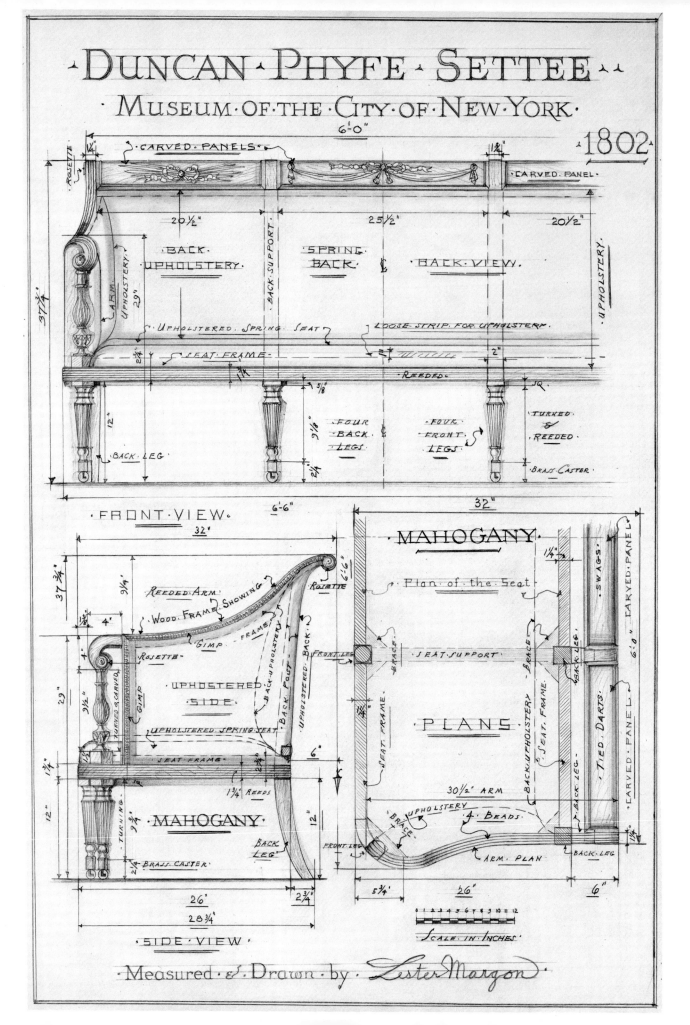

DUNCAN · PHYFE · SETTEE

· MUSEUM · OF · THE · CITY · OF · NEW · YORK ·

· 1802 ·

6'-0"

· CARVED · PANELS ·

1¾"

· CARVED · PANEL ·

ROSETTE

20½"   25½"   20½"

· BACK · UPHOLSTERY ·   · SPRING · BACK ·   · BACK · VIEW ·

UPHOLSTERY · 29"

· ARM ·

BACK · SUPPORT

UPHOLSTERY

· UPHOLSTERED · SPRING · SEAT ·   · LOOSE · STRIP · FOR · UPHOLSTERY ·

· SEAT · FRAME ·   2¾"   1¼"   2"

REEDED

5/8"

· FOUR · BACK · LEGS ·   · FOUR · FRONT · LEGS ·   · TURNED · & · REEDED ·

12"   9⅛"

· BACK · LEG ·   2¼"   · BRASS · CASTER ·

FRONT · VIEW ·   6'-6"

32"   32"   · MAHOGANY ·

· Plan · of · the · Seat ·

1¼"

SWAGS

CARVED · PANEL

37¾"   9¾"

· REEDED · ARM ·   SHOWING   ROSETTE

6'-6"

· WOOD · FRAME ·

GIMP   FRAME ·

ROSETTE

29"   9½"

· UPHOLSTERED · SIDE ·

BACK · UPHOLSTERY   UPHOLSTERED · BACK ·

BACK · POST ·

FRONT · LEG ·   BRACE   · SEAT · SUPPORT ·

SEAT · FRAME ·

· PLANS ·

· BACK · UPHOLSTERY ·

BRACE

SEAT · FRAME ·

BACK · LEG

TIED · DARTS ·

CARVED · PANEL

6'-0"   CARVED · PANEL

GIMP

TURNED · & · CARVED

· UPHOLSTERED · SPRING · SEAT ·

· SEAT · FRAME ·   2¾"   6"

1¾"   REEDS   12"

12"   9¾"   · MAHOGANY ·

· TURNING ·

· BACK · LEG ·

1¼"   30½" · ARM

UPHOLSTERY   · 4 · BEADS ·

BRACE

FRONT · LEG   BACK · LEG

2¼"   · BRASS · CASTER ·   · ARM · PLAN ·   5¾"   26"   6"

26"   2¾"

28¾"

· SIDE · VIEW ·

0 1 2 3 4 5 6 7 8 9 10 11 12

· SCALE · IN · INCHES ·

· Measured · & · Drawn · by · Lester Margon ·

DUNCAN PHYFE SETTEE
Museum of the City of New York

In the Museum of the City of New York is installed a drawing room from an early 19th century house formerly located on Greenwich Street. Most of the furniture in this room was made by Duncan Phyfe, including the magnificent settee as shown. It is made of rich mahogany. This seating piece is done in his best style under the influence of Thomas Sheraton. Of particular interest is the graceful profile of the front posts and the irrational way the arms turn inward at the handhold. This is a treatment that has not been repeated in any other settees. As usual there are three carved panels along the upper back consisting of swags at the center and tied darts at each side. The carving is in low relief, crisp and sparkling. The settee is upholstered in green striped satin. The arms are a continuous curve with reeding on the top edge and ending in a slight scroll. The seat frame is also reeded. There are eight legs, turned and reeded, with brass casters. The arm supports are turned, reeded and carved. These settees are priceless. Even good reproductions are rare and costly. Much of the brilliance of the work of Duncan Phyfe is due to his careful selection of Santo Domingo mahogany. He often paid fabulous sums for the logs and supervised the cutting of the veneers. Seldom using contrasting woods except for inlaid borders, he depended solely on the brilliance of mahogany to achieve the desired effects.

THE DUNCAN PHYFE ROOM

The Henry Francis du Pont Winterthur Museum

It is indeed a rare occasion to see a room full of the furniture of Duncan Phyfe. Included are side and armchairs, a window seat, side tables, a settee, a globe stand, a console and a drop-leaf center table. There is an upholstered easy-chair and the elegant harpsichord. With the furniture, gracefully placed, note the elegant window draperies and the crystal chandeliers and wall-brackets, the tall mirror and the two portraits of fair ladies. The oriental rug is exemplary. What a wealth of craftsmanship to enjoy and appreciate. It was between 1785 and 1840 that America established the Federal form of government. Robert Adam, in England, sponsored the Antique style, inspired by the excavations in Pompeii and Herculaneum. Emphasis was put on graceful lines, delicate carving and painted decoration on furniture. Duncan Phyfe was the leading exponent in America, and his work was the epitome of perfection.

DUNCAN PHYFE SOFA
Detroit Institute of Arts

Duncan Phyfe made many sofas of different sizes and various designs. This Sheraton-style model was the most popular, possibly due to its refinement and restraint. As Phyfe was always striving to improve his output, even this model was due for many changes. In comparing the measured drawing from the Museum of the City of New York with the photograph from the Detroit Institute of Arts, these differences will become apparent: Whereas the carved back panels remained the same, the reeded seat frame was supplanted by upholstery and the turnings are different. Perhaps the main difference is the treatment of the arm at the handhold. Both models are in mahogany from the beginning of the 19th century. This desire for continual change was one of Duncan Phyfe's best characteristics. He tried to satisfy the demands of his patrons and keep abreast of the changes of the times. This was very well until he began working in the Empire style, which proved to be his defeat.

McINTIRE · TIP-TOP · TABLE ·

· PHILADELPHIA · MUSEUM · of · ART ·

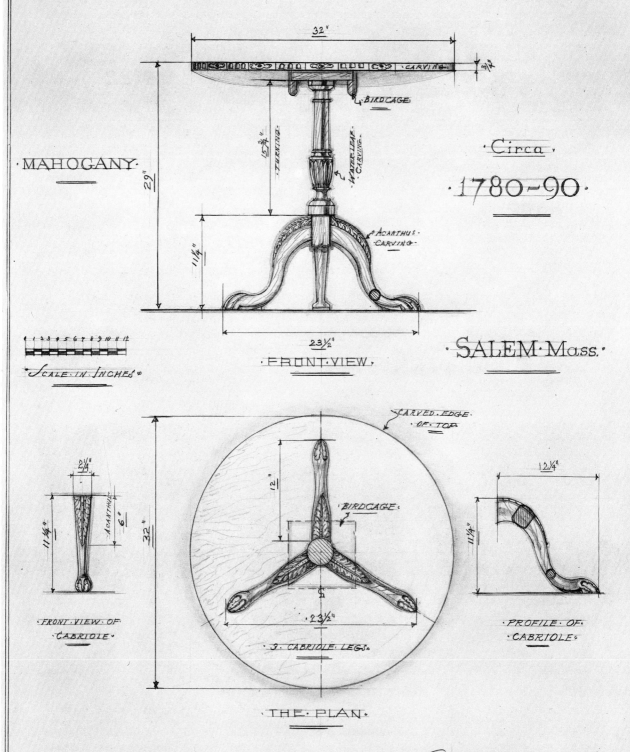

MAHOGANY

· Circa ·
· 1780~90 ·

· SALEM · Mass. ·

32"

3/4"

· BIRDCAGE ·

· TURNING ·

· WATER · LEAF ·
· CARVING ·

· ACANTHUS ·
· CARVING ·

29"

15 3/4"

11 1/4"

23 1/2"

· FRONT · VIEW ·

· SCALE · IN · INCHES ·

· CARVED · EDGE ·
· OF · TOP ·

2 1/4"

11 1/4"

6"

· ACANTHUS ·

· FRONT · VIEW · OF ·
· CABRIOLE ·

12"

· BIRDCAGE ·

32"

23 1/2"

· 3 · CABRIOLE · LEGS ·

· THE · PLAN ·

12 1/4"

11 1/4"

· PROFILE · OF ·
· CABRIOLE ·

Measured · & · Drawn · by · Lester Margon ·

McINTIRE TILT-TOP TABLE
Philadelphia Museum of Art

This Adam mahogany tilt-top table is from Salem, Massachusetts, *circa* 1780-1790. It was carved by Samuel McIntire. It is indeed a most delightful table. The ultra-refinement of the design, the crispness of the carving and the slender cabriole legs make it a superb piece. There has been so much controversy as to whether or not McIntire was actually a carver. After intensive investigation it was finally decided that he not only did much of the carving himself but actually carved furniture for other cabinetmakers. This is one of the treasures of the Philadelphia Museum of Art. As the bulletin states – "Rising high on the Acropolis of Fairmount, the majestic structure dominates the skyline for many miles around. Aesthetically also, it dominates the art horizon of the city and extends its influence far, far beyond – for this magnificent Museum, covering 10 acres and housing 100,000 works of art, is one of the great museums of the world."

PEMBROKE TABLE

The Wadsworth Atheneum, Hartford, Connecticut

This mahogany Chippendale Pembroke table, *circa* 1750-1780, has two drop leaves. This is certainly a most skillful rendition with the beautifully pierced stretchers and corner brackets. The gracefully shaped top adds much to its attractiveness. There are two drawers approachable from either side. The shaping of the Marlborough square legs is articulate and the addition of the gadroon carving gives the table a certain distinction. Nothing has been left out and nothing could be added. The design is complete. It is the work of a brilliant artisan who knew when to stop. During this period Pembroke tables found favor in the bedroom where breakfast could be served unobtrusively. It was a utility table to be found in any room of the house. This table was probably made in Philadelphia.

McINTIRE HEPPLEWHITE SIDE CHAIR

Los Angeles County Museum of Art

A splendid example of New England furniture in California is this side chair attributed to Samuel McIntire of Salem, Massachusetts. It is made of mahogany of the shield-back variety, *circa* 1800. It is in the collection of decorative arts of the Los Angeles County Museum of Art. It has all the required credentials, and the spokes of the shield are beautifully carved. There is no doubt that McIntire designed furniture which was executed in his own workshop. That he was a carver

of exceptional talents is evident in the many examples of his work. His sofas are exceptionally brilliant performances of which he was particularly fond. His chairs are great in number but they all have a certain similarity which immediately identifies them as his work. His favored carvings consisted of baskets of fruit and flowers, festoons, drapery, eagles, a cluster of grapes, cornucopias and Adam-type sprays of laurel.

SHERATON·INFLUENCE·SOFA·

METROPOLITAN·MUSEUM·OF·ART·

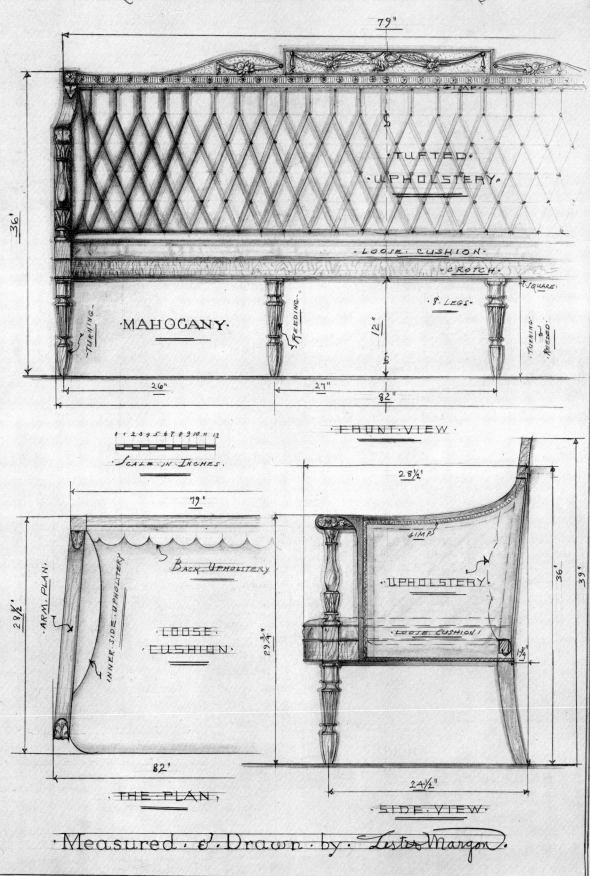

79"

36'

TUFTED·
·UPHOLSTERY·

·LOOSE·CUSHION·

·CROTCH·

·SQUARE·

·TURNING·

MAHOGANY·

·REEDING·

·8·LEGS·

·TURNING·&·REEDED·

12"

26"   27"

82"

·FRONT·VIEW·

0 1 2 3 4 5 6 7 8 9 10 11 12
·SCALE·IN·INCHES·

79"

28½'

28½'

·ARM·PLAN·

·INNER·SIDE·UPHOLSTERY·

·BACK·UPHOLSTERY·

LOOSE·
CUSHION·

29¾"

GIMP·

·UPHOLSTERY·

·LOOSE·CUSHION·

1¾"

36'

39"

82"

·THE·PLAN·

24½"

·SIDE·VIEW·

Measured·&·Drawn·by·Lester Margon·

SHERATON INFLUENCE SOFA

Metropolitan Museum of Art   Fletcher Fund

This Sheraton Influence sofa in mahogany, of the late 18th century, was probably made in Salem, Massachusetts. It is almost identical with a sofa attributed to Samuel McIntire, with one exception. Instead of the carved spread eagle in the central upper panel there is a carved basket of fruit, which was his favorite subject. The carving and the detail are so exquisite that they might well have been the handiwork of the master carver. This may be seen in so many of the Salem houses whose interiors he designed. This ele-

gant sofa has been recently reupholstered in a ruby velvet in tufted fashion. It now appears like a breath of fresh air in the rather staid gallery of the American Wing of the Metropolitan Museum of Art. At first glance it was a shock but on second viewing it proved what can be done to give new life to a splendid antique. It would be interesting to compare this sofa with the work of Duncan Phyfe of the same period to appreciate their likeness and differences.

DUNCAN HOUSE PARLOR

Metropolitan Museum of Art, New York

This room is from Haverhill, Massachusetts. The Duncan House was erected in 1818. Here we see a typical seaport home of the Early Republic. The Adam tradition forms the basis of the design. The cornice is typical of the period, based upon the works of Asher Benjamin. The richly colored scenic wallpaper gives character to the parlor. It is a French paper and tells the story of a hunt from its start at the chateau to the finish. The furniture here is New England Hepplewhite and Sheraton. Much of this fine furniture was made in the vicinity of Boston. It carried out the popular taste for light tones in the woods, often using satinwood and burl maple veneers. The sofa shown is covered in satin showing an early 19th century preference for stripes and tiny stars. This is indeed an elegant parlor. The house later became Brown's Tavern and then the Eagle House.

SHERATON ARMCHAIR

Detroit Institute of Arts

This superb Sheraton armchair in mahogany is from the State of New York, *circa* 1795. After arriving in London in 1790, Sheraton published "The Cabinet-Maker and Upholsterer's Drawing Book," in 1791. He designed much furniture which was made by other cabinetmakers. His influence was widespread, especially in America. Many of his designs of chairs were especially beautiful. He favored the square back and this model is an excellent example of his style. Particularly interesting is the central arched form supported by the pierced center splat in the form of an urn, supplemented at the top by the three feathers. Otherwise the chair is typical, with the graceful arms and the shaped arm supports. The tapered legs have spade feet. The brocade upholstery is of the period. This gracious model is in the collection of the Detroit Institute of Arts.

LIST OF ILLUSTRATIONS

(Asterisks indicate photographs accompanied by measured drawings.)

PHILADELPHIA CABINETMAKERS

William Penn squired a group of workers from the Rhine Valley, who settled in the vicinity of Philadelphia. From 1683, this city became the principal center of cabinetmaking. Of course, there were many other places where furniture was being made. These boasted such excellent designers and cabinetmakers as John Goddard of Rhode Island, the Townsends of Newport and John Seymour of Boston. However, this country has never had such a sudden explosion of talent as was asesmbled in Philadelphia about the middle of the 18th century. The work of these designers was of the highest quality and the productivity tremendous. It was original in conception and surpassed the work of the English. It remains the undisputed epitome of the finest workmanship.

THE foremost Philadelphia cabinetmakers of that period were: Thomas Affleck, William Savery, James Gillingham, Jonathan Shoemaker, Benjamin Randolph, Jonathan Gostelowe and a host of equally proficient workers.

In the spring of 1935 the Pennsylvania Museum of Art held a Loan Exhibition of authenticated furniture of the great Philadelphia cabinetmakers. It included the work of forty craftsmen represented by furniture and relics. This brief summary will not permit going into detail concerning the outputs of all these worthy gentlemen. Therefore, only a few of the most noted have been selected for further consideration. They are William Savery, Benjamin Randolph, Thomas Affleck and Jonathan Gostelowe.

These Philadelphia cabinetmakers produced the finest furniture that has ever been made in America. Featured were the elaborate chests of drawers, secretaries, lowboys, chairs and flamboyant Rococo highboys. The latter featured, from 1765 to 1780, carving that reached its finest perfection. This furniture was masterfully executed, incorporating much of the richness of the Chippendale style, including Rococo carving, elaborate decoration and perfection in execution. The work of these designers was most skillful and artistic. There is little comparison between these Philadelphia highboys and anything ever produced in England. They are indisputably the supreme creations of the period. The nobility of design, the perfection of the execution and the innate sense for excellence in design are beyond compare.

The splendor and high character of these Philadelphia highboys have created such a tremendous demand that prices now have escalated to such a point that they are astronomical. One highboy, it is known, brought $44,000 at an auction. Most of these examples are in museum collections.

Every part of these highboys is expertly executed. The aprons are cut in cyma curves and carved streamers flow in graceful lineation. Flowers, leaves, urns, finials and pendants are exquisitely carved, including fanciful cartouches. A feature of these pieces is the variety of the plans, including bow, serpentine, oxbow and block fronts.

Featured in these highboys are such items as scrolled pediments perforated at the center by carved rosettes, flaming vases, finials, friezes of applied Chippendale fretwork, and carved festoons of flowers, drapery and stalactites. There are usually five small drawers toward the top and three larger ones below. Pilasters are fluted and corners chamfered, decorated with encrustments of carved leaves and flowers. Many of the cases retain the original brasses with bail handles. These were often of good size and elaborate. Although much embellishment was manifest, the elegance of proportions and the insistence upon proper restraint are evident. The lowboys are of various types with one long drawer at the top and smaller drawers at the sides. They have cabriole or turned legs with shaped stretchers. Many have carved aprons featuring shell motifs held in place by sprays of leaves and flowers. The cabriole legs are often short and carved with acanthus forms.

While profuse carving predominated on many of these pieces, it should be understood that careful study and restrained treatment were mandatory. The paucity of such carving does not mean that the cabinetmaker lacked the necessary skills. It largely depended upon the intent of the design. That these Philadelphia cabinet-makers were masters in determining the placement of carving is evident in their products.

In the 18th century, the beauty and durability of mahogany, the rich patterns of the veneers, the grain, the rich coloring and the exotic lustre, made it the preferred wood. This was especially true because the carvings could be executed with the minutest details generally associated with the jeweler's artistry. For these reasons Chippendale chose carving as his main recourse for decoration.

There is little more that need be said in praise of the work of these Philadelphia cabinetmakers. Their work is superb and remains as examples of excellent design and masterful accomplishment.

WILLIAM SAVERY

William Savery was born in 1721 and married in 1742. He was practically unknown until a label bearing his name was discovered on a lowboy in the Van Cortlandt Manor in New York City, which read — "All sorts of chairs and joiner's work, made and sold at the Sign of the Chair. Below Market in Second Street, Philadelphia." He is known to have made highboys, lowboys, bureaux, arm and side chairs, daybeds and desks, mostly in the Chippendale style. Savery was a Quaker. At his demise, an inventory of his estate included no carving tools. Therefore, it can be assumed that he had others do his carving. This was customary with many of the Philadelphia cabinetmakers. Early pieces show that he worked in the Queen Anne style. Examples of his furniture may be seen in the Winterthur Museum, The Detroit Institute of Arts and the Philadelphia Museum of Art as well as at the Henry Ford Museum at Dearborn. He is considered one of the outstanding cabinetmakers of his day. He died in 1788.

BENJAMIN RANDOLPH

Benjamin Randolph was born in Monmouth County, New Jersey in 1730. As early as 1762 he was established in business at the shop "Golden Eagle," located on Chestnut Street. He did extensive advertising. His labels read as follows — "All sorts of Cabinet and Chair Work made and sold by Benj. Randolph," adding his shop location. He wrote a receipt book now in the collection of the Winterthur Museum. The Philadelphia Exhibition in 1935 included two side chairs and a tall clock-case now in the Pennsylvania Hospital. Considered one of the foremost cabinetmakers, six "sample chairs" displayed his skill in carving. These were in the Chippendale style, with carved perforated backs with extended "ears." The back supports were decorated with intricate floral carving. Examples of his work may be seen in the M. and M. Karolik Collection of the Museum of Fine Arts in Boston. Thomas Jefferson is believed to have commissioned him to make a table on which the Declaration of Independence was written. He retired from business in 1780 and died in 1790.

THOMAS AFFLECK

Born in 1740 in Aberdeen, Scotland, Thomas Affleck emigrated to America in 1763. Before arriving in this country he served an apprenticeship in England. His shop was located on Second Street at Lowne's Alley. He specialized in the making of beautiful furniture in the Chinese Chippendale style. His clientele were among the foremost and richest families in Philadelphia. Considered one of the foremost and most popular cabinetmakers of his times, his output was tremendous, as was evidenced by the huge occupational tax which he was required to pay. One of the finest examples of his work is a highboy in the collection at the Pendleton House of the Rhode Island School of Design Museum. It is in walnut, *circa* 1759. Typical of these Philadelphia pieces, the hooded top has a broken arch in front. The rest of the top is flat. So many pieces have been attributed to Thomas Affleck that it is impossible to verify their authenticity. He died in 1795.

JONATHAN GOSTELOWE

Born in 1745 at Passyunk, Pennsylvania, Jonathan Gostelowe was an apprentice to George Claypoole, 1762, where he learned his trade. After a busy career, he retired in 1793. His shop was located at No. 66 Market Street. He then sold his entire stock at auction, consisting of mahogany furniture, chairs, tables, washing stands and bedsteads. A Chippendale walnut chest of drawers dated 1790 was discovered in the Philadelphia Museum of Art. It has a serpentine front, the corners are chamfered and fluted and it has shaped ogee-bracket feet. His masterpiece is said to be a "Wedding Bureau and Mirror" which he made for Elizabeth Tower. There are examples of his work in the Williamsburg Restoration. Jonathan Gostelowe died February 3, 1795.

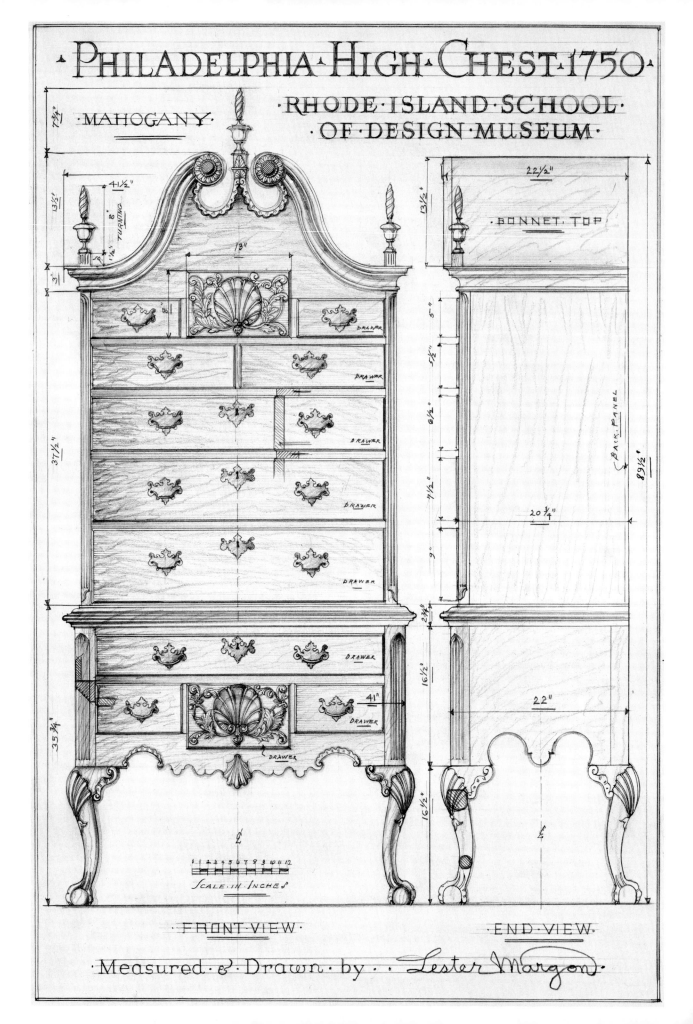

PHILADELPHIA·HIGH·CHEST·1750·

·MAHOGANY·

·RHODE·ISLAND·SCHOOL·
OF·DESIGN·MUSEUM·

7¾"

13½'

4½"
8"
1½" TURNING

3"

13"

22½"

·BONNET·TOP·

13½'

DRAWER

DRAWER

5"

5½"

DRAWER

6½"

37½'

DRAWER

7½"

BACK·PANEL

DRAWER

9"

20¾"

8½'

2¾"

DRAWER

16½'

35¾"

DRAWER

41"

22"

DRAWER

16½'

16½'

0·1·2·3·4·5·6·7·8·9·10·11·12
·SCALE·IN·INCHES·

·FRONT·VIEW·

·END·VIEW·

·Measured·&·Drawn·by·· Lester Margon·

PHILADELPHIA HIGH CHEST

The Rhode Island School of Design, Providence

This Philadelphia high chest in mahogany, *circa* 1750, is certainly one of the grandest examples of the cabinetmaker's craft. It possesses many of the grandiose attributes that recommend it as a masterpiece of this most resplendent period. It is attributed to Thomas Affleck of Philadelphia. He is considered one of the foremost cabinetmakers who produced the finest furniture in the Chippendale style. The bonnet top is broken for the inclusion of a flame-like turned finial. The center scrolls are ornamented with floral carving, displaying his excellent skill as a carver. Perhaps the most auspicious part of the design is the two carved panel drawer fronts with the shell motif at the center surrounded by elegant acanthus scrolls. Note that the shell carvings are concave in the vertical section to afford the necessary depth and dramatic effect. The various sized drawers add much to the complexity of the design. This magnificent high chest is in the collection of the Rhode Island School of Design Museum in Providence. It was necessary to secure special permission from the Director to include this measured drawing in this volume. The Museum occupies the elegant Pendleton Mansion.

PHILADELPHIA HIGHBOY
The Henry Francis du Pont Winterthur Museum

There were a great number of Philadelphia high-boys made, *circa* 1765-1780. Of these, a great number were similar in design and treatment. Many were attributed to well-known cabinetmakers while others, equally efficient, must remain name-less. In the Chippendale style, when the Rococo demanded the utmost of skill, the results were often quite different. In some instances the carv-ings on these mahogany highboys were inade-quate, ill-placed and sadly disposed. These highboys required the ultimate in judgment, ex-perience and performance. The lavish designs had to be discreetly co-ordinated and it required vast experience to evaluate the extensive ornamenta-tion. The curved pediments had to be just right to conform with the varied lines of the base. It was not a simple matter. That so many of the cabinetmakers succeeded eminently is proof of their skill and ability. In many instances the per-formance was equal to the task. This splendid Philadelphia highboy is in the collection of the Henry Francis du Pont Winterthur Museum.

"HOWE" HIGHBOY

Philadelphia Museum of Art

One of the great pieces of Philadelphia Chippendale furniture has long been known as the "Howe" Highboy. Made of mahogany, its date is *circa* 1770. The Fox and Grape fable motif is carved on the lower central drawer panel. Of superb elegance is the double scrolled pediment with the pierced bracing, ending in the carved scrolls. At the center is a vase overflowing with flowers. The ends are surmounted by carved vase finials holding flowers. The cornice is not a feature but serves well as a base for the pediment. On the end corners are carved drops of leaves and flowers. The pierced pulls and escutcheon plates of brass are extraordinary. The rather short cabriole legs are carved at the knee and sweep toward the floor ending in ball-and-claw feet. The crotch is brilliant. What more can be said in praise of this magnificent example of Philadelphia design and cabinet work? The highboy is in the collection of the Philadelphia Museum of Art.

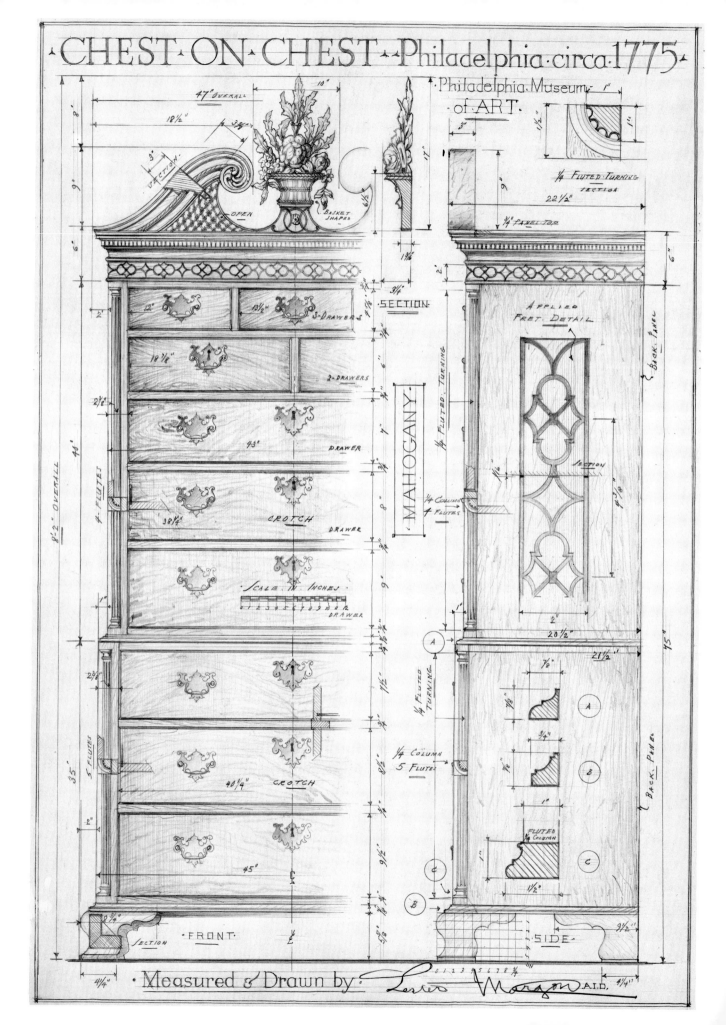

CHEST·ON·CHEST·Philadelphia·circa·1775·

Philadelphia·Museum·
of·ART·

¼ FLUTED TURNING

·MAHOGANY·

SECTION

·Scale in Inches·

APPLIED
FRET DETAIL

·FRONT·

·SIDE·

·Measured & Drawn by· *Lester Margon* A.I.D.

CHEST ON CHEST

Philadelphia Museum of Art
Purchase of the Elizabeth S. Shippen Fund

Particularly of Philadelphia, this mahogany Chippendale chest on chest is attributed to Jonathan Gostelowe. The date is *circa* 1775. The piece is certainly magnificent and would fit gracefully into the great houses of the period. In studying this piece we can well appreciate the profound artistry of the Philadelphia cabinetmakers. The date itself is eclectic, 1775, when the thirteen Colonies were about to become a nation. The work produced at this time in Philadelphia is the finest product of Americana. The spirit is so excellently exemplified in this chest on chest. Certainly, the design elements originated in England but they were so eminently developed and enhanced in this country, with more graceful lines and attributes that make it distinctively American. Crowned with a flamboyant broken pediment, the bonnet top is further elaborated by a basket of oak leaves at the center. This is indeed an unorthodox bravura performance in the crowning glory of the citadel. Taking the chest on chest in its particular details, mention should be made of the double scrolled top with the accompanying grill work, culminating in the volute, which is decorated by the carved rosettes. In the cornice is the conventional Chippendale geometric pattern only 1/16″ raised from the surface. One could go on and on picking out particular details of rare excellence in this splendid Philadelphia masterpiece.

PHILADELPHIA HIGHBOY

Metropolitan Museum af Art   Kennedy Fund, 1918

One of the grandest highboys made in Philadelphia *circa* 1765, is shown in the drawing room of the Powell House at the Metropolitan Museum of Art in New York. It is of Chippendale inspiration but the excellence of the space-divisions and the brilliance of the carving are beyond compare. The elegance of the double scroll top which is pierced by the placement of the sculptured female bust, and the classicism of the urn finials at the top are masterly. All portions of the design are brought together harmoniously. The carving of the lower drawer panel is superb. These Philadelphia highboys are paramount in artistry and skill. These pieces surpass anything produced in England. This one is a *tour de force* of which we can be justly proud. The richness of the mahogany veneers and the handling of the carved cabriole legs are superlative. This is a piece that thwarts any fair description. It is the ultimate in furniture design.

ORNAMENTED HIGHBOY

The Henry Francis du Pont Winterthur Museum

The pediment of this mahogany Philadelphia highboy is particularly splendid. Made in the Chippendale style, *circa* 1765-1780, it presents a picture of opulence seldom approached. The scrolled pediment pictured with rosettes at the inner ends, and the two flaming finials are exemplary. The applied carving below the top features a radiating central motif which serves as the base for extending scrolls. On the lower central drawer is a carved shell with accompanying scrolls. The

mahogany is straight grained. There are eight drawers of varying sizes in the upper portion of the chest and four drawers in the stand. The short cabriole legs are carved at the knee, with the usual ball-and-claw feet. The crowning glory of this Philadelphia highboy is the central carved ornament at the center top. It defies description. It is just the right touch of gallantry. This highboy is in the Henry Francis du Pont Winterthur Museum.

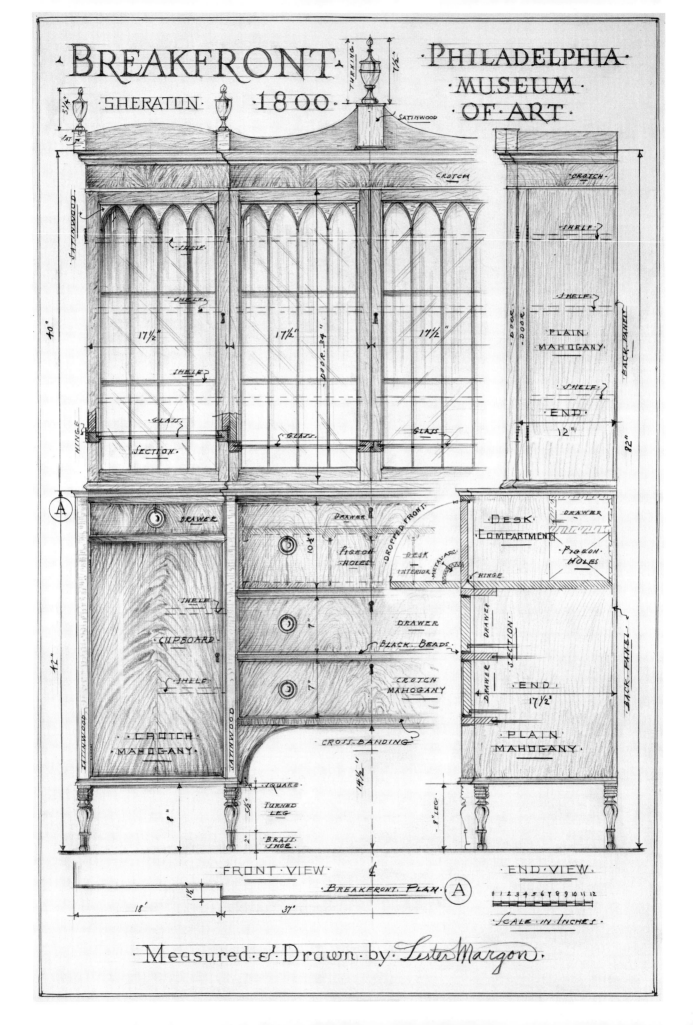

BREAKFRONT

PHILADELPHIA MUSEUM OF ART

SHERATON 1800

FRONT VIEW

END VIEW

BREAKFRONT PLAN Ⓐ

SCALE IN INCHES

0 1 2 3 4 5 6 7 8 9 10 11 12

Measured & Drawn by Lester Margon

BREAKFRONT

Philadelphia Museum of Art

This magnificent Sheraton style breakfront in mahogany with satinwood trimmings, dates from *circa* 1800. The locality is Massachusetts. Here is a combination bookcase and desk compartment with drawers and cupboard compartments. It is supported by six turned legs of splendid design with brass shoes. When the desk front is lowered, a collection of drawers and pigeon-holes is revealed. The sombreness of the huge mass of mahogany is relieved by the clever addition of panels of satinwood. At the top are a series of delightful urn finials which are jewel-like in perfection. What makes this breakfront so distinctive is the Gothic arched divisions of the glass doors of the book-case. The fire and matching of the crotch mahogany veneers is breathtaking. The entire piece is alive. Note that the bookcase top is set back to create the proper perspective. Seldom is such a big piece made to appear so light and graceful, due to the clever manipulation of line, mass, woods and knowledgeable designs. The break in the front is another factor that adds to its credibility. Despite the many lines of the fret of the glass doors of the bookcase, the china shown installed on the shelves shows up well. This is indeed one of the many treasures to be found in the Philadelphia Museum of Art.

237

BANISTER-BACK CHAIR

Metropolitan Museum of Art
Gift of Mrs. Russell Sage, 1909

This banister-back walnut armchair, *circa* 1725, features the Flemish scroll type of carved crest, splendid turnings and back-post finials. It has Spanish feet which seem to belong to a later date. It is in the American Wing of the Metropolitan Museum of Art. Its sophisticated design does not go particularly well with the crude rush seat. Of course, cushions were always used with such chairs. The influence of the Restoration is evident, for the finer residences were built in the Renaissance style. This armchair might be considered transitional, for it combines the earlier banister-type back with the later academic tracery. This period was erratic. It borrowed from the past and incorporated forms that were anticipated. The chair is stately but it somehow appears incongruous. This is an excellent model for comparison.

HEPPLEWHITE SIDE CHAIR

Detroit Institute of Arts

There are so many different examples of Hepplewhite shield-back chairs, but this model is one of the finest. Made in mahogany, the date is *circa* 1780-1800. George Hepplewhite favored the French furniture of Louis XV and Louis XVI styles. However, his chairs were more carefully proportioned and the detail worked out with greater care. His influence was great, especially in America, where it seemed to fit graciously into the trend of the Federal period. In this model the pierced center splat of the shield is delightfully delineated with drapery, carved husk forms and floral motifs climaxing at the top with fan lineation, all held together at the base by a carved rosette. The graceful shape of the seat front and the square tapered legs all add to the refinement of the chair. This model is in the collection of the Detroit Institute of Arts.

WILLIAM & MARY HIGHBOY

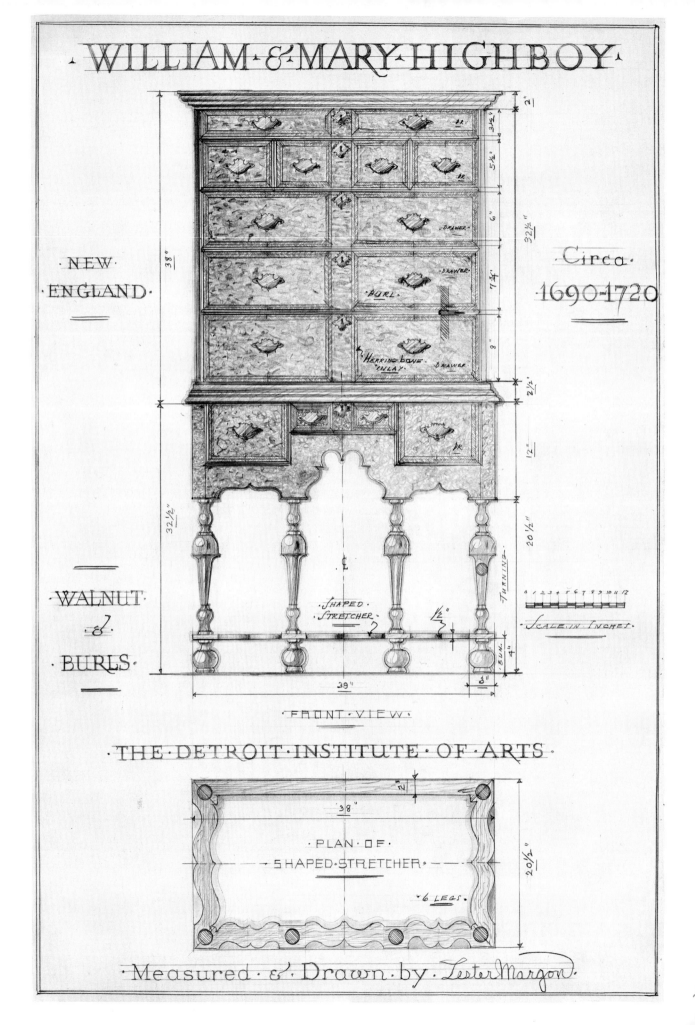

NEW
ENGLAND

Circa
1690-1720

WALNUT
&
BURLS

BURL

HERRING-BONE
INLAY

DRAWER

SHAPED
STRETCHER

TURNING

BUN

SCALE IN INCHES

38"

FRONT · VIEW

THE · DETROIT · INSTITUTE · OF · ARTS

38"

PLAN · OF
SHAPED · STRETCHER

6 LEGS

20½"

Measured · & · Drawn · by · Lester Margon

WILLIAM AND MARY HIGHBOY

The Detroit Institute of Arts

This William and Mary highboy, *circa* 1690-1720, from New England, is one of the grandest of its kind. The contrast of walnut with the burl veneers, enhanced by the herring-bone borders around the drawers produces the effect of a rich tapestry. It is indeed a masterpiece in the space divisions, the compact proportions and the superb lineation. The use of burl on the drawer fronts appears only on the finest highboys of the period. The cornice and the substantial mouldings dividing the lower section from the drawers above are well defined. The beautifully shaped stretcher holds the six legs in place and is in itself a part of the decorative design. Note how the central arched form of the apron produces a sense of levitation to the otherwise seemingly heavy bulk as well as adding grace to the entire design. The trumpet turnings are eloquent in their stately demeanor. This is indeed a highboy to view and ponder, for it was made only a century after the landing of the Pilgrim Fathers. This highboy would be a remarkable feat for even a much later date. The value of such a highboy today is unpredictable. It is one of the treasures of the Detroit Institute of Arts.

THE "MAUSE" HIGHBOY

The Henry Francis du Pont Winterthur Museum

The cabinetmaker Joseph Hosner of Concord, Massachusetts was born December 27, 1735. He learned his craft from Robert Rosier, a Frenchman. From 1761 he worked steadily at cabinetmaking. Hosner's furniture ranged from country versions of the Chippendale style to more sophisticated designs. The "Mause" highboy, as it was called, was made for the Reverend William Emerson and later owned by Ralph Waldo Emerson. This highboy of cherry and maple, *circa* 1770, is perched on tall slender cabriole legs that seem almost too delicate to support the mass above. Of special interest is the center block-front panel which is made from a solid piece of wood and applied. Note the curious little sunken panel beneath the carved sunburst and the doge attached at the center. This pyramidal highboy is in the collection of the Henry Francis du Pont Winterthur Museum.

HIGH CHEST OF DRAWERS

The Henry Francis du Pont Winterthur Museum

In the joiner's bill enumerating the veneers and inlay used in the making of fine furniture in Massachusetts before 1750, are mentioned "Stringed, feneered, stars and scalups." This high chest of drawers of white wood and white walnut, Massachusetts, *circa* 1725-1740, has inlays of birch to accentuate the stars and the inlaid sunbursts at the top and bottom. The stringed inlay beneath the top forms a border for the hood and drawers. The brasses do seem a bit small. However, the high chest of drawers is impressive with the graceful line of the broken pediment and the inclusion of the flamelike top finials. The lower apron is broken to permit the placement of the acorn drops. The simple finely shaped cabriole legs seem to be just right. Note that the sunburst inlays are applied in sunken panels, which adds to their effectiveness. This high chest of drawers is in the collection of the Henry Francis du Pont Winterthur Museum.

243

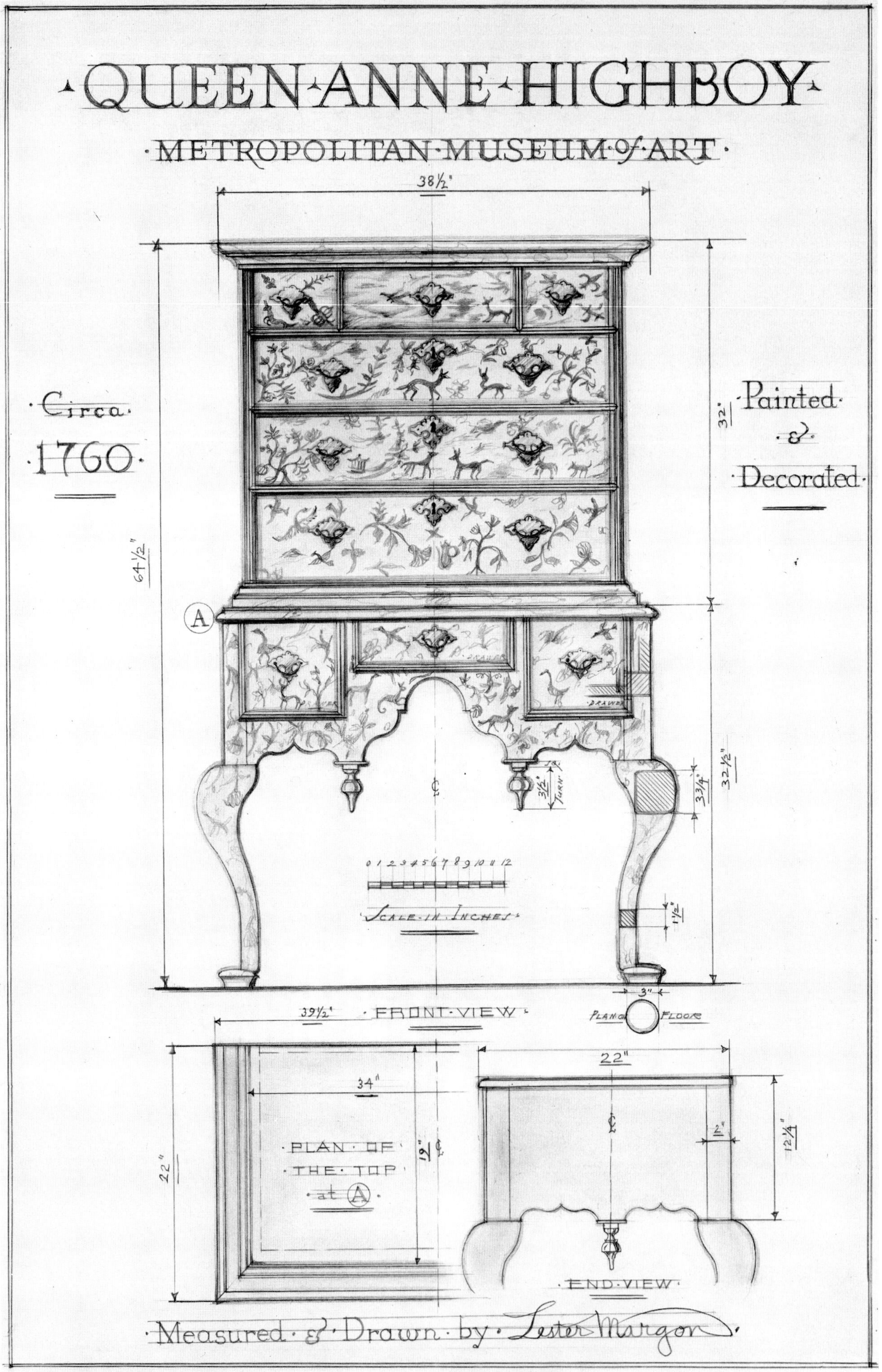

QUEEN ANNE HIGHBOY

METROPOLITAN MUSEUM of ART

Circa
1760

Painted
&
Decorated

38½"

32"

64½"

Ⓐ

32½"

3½"
TURN.

3¾"

1½"

0 1 2 3 4 5 6 7 8 9 10 11 12

Scale in Inches

C̶L̶

3"

PLAN OF FLOOR

FRONT VIEW

39½"

34"

22"

19½"

22"

PLAN OF
THE TOP
at Ⓐ

22"

12¼"

2"

END VIEW

Measured & Drawn by Lester Margon

HIGHBOY IN TWO PARTS

Metropolitan Museum of Art, New York   *Gift of Mrs. J. Insley Blair, 1946*

This rather unusual highboy, in two parts, is in the Queen Anne style. Made of maple and pine, it is painted brown on black. The painted decoration is a mixture of the Oriental and the provincial. The birds and the animals seem to be having a very good time. The highboy is probably from Connecticut, *circa* 1760. Beside the unusual decorative treatment in monochrome, the highboy is noteworthy by reason of its preposterous cabriole legs. Not alone are they unorthodox but they are lacking in demeanor. The huge bulge at the knee descending to a small round section to be confronted by the inadequate pigeon feet does not seem adequate to support the bulk above. Then too, the upper chest of drawers on the lowboy base appears to be contrived. It is the inappropriateness throughout the entire piece that makes it interesting if not tending to invite favor.

PENNSYLVANIA GERMAN DRESSER

The Philadelphia Museum of Art

The furniture made by the Pennsylvania German settlers, *circa* 1730-1750, was well proportioned and always colorful. This dresser was originally painted a startling red and yellow. Time fortunately has toned it down into harmonious tones. The scallops on the upper section are incised and painted. On the lower case they are boldly carved. A handsome cornice adds to the unusual character of the piece. The two-door glass-enclosed shelving is for the display of treasured pottery. There is a working surface below. Beneath are three small drawers and a two-door cupboard for storage. The work was done by the people and the colors were homemade. Despite their tendency toward asceticism, dislike for worldly progress and mechanical invention, the Pennsylvania Germans lived a hearty and wholesome life. They were a subjective people, and the family was the unit of their existence: Let disturbers beware. However, they made a worthy contribution to American furniture design.

CHEST ON A STAND

Old Sturbridge Village

This Queen Anne chest on a stand from Massachusetts, *circa* 1750, is from the Village Furniture Collection of Old Sturbridge Village. The torus and the cornice form a shallow drawer. Below are six drawers of varied sizes. Cyma curves accentuate the shaped skirt supported by cabriole legs with pad feet. This early date may be an excuse for crudity and subsequent limitations of the design. Certainly the extended apron appears to be on the heavy side and the cornice seems to be a bit meagre. However, it is just these evident discrepancies that make this peasant furniture so engaging. Correctness can become distressing if carried to an unwarranted degree. These local joiners just made what they felt was right and what could be more engrossing?

YESTERDAY, TODAY AND TOMORROW

O URS is a young country that has made magnificent progress, but perfection, the betterment of life for everyone in our country, must always be our goal. Whether for better or for worse, radical changes in our social, political, and economic structures have already occurred, and at the same time have created the mood for a new approach to furniture design. Prior to the several last decades the designer studied the period styles and reproduced them more or less faithfully. There was little attempt at, or demand for, the production of anything new. Now, due to the changes in our outlook, we tend to evaluate things differently.

Wanting to be "contemporary," many people try to dissociate themselves from the past. But although the dominant urge in recent years has been to design something new and different, among many there is a growing mood of appreciation for the beautiful things that are our heritage, so accessible as to have been long overlooked. Young people join with older ones who have never neglected the beautiful work of American craftsmen.

Let us hope that this trend will grow, and will produce a harmony of the best of the old and the best of the new. Unfortunately, because of the limitations of the machine and the need for mass production to satisfy the demands of the population explosion, the making of individual handcrafted pieces of furniture is no longer feasible for most. The training of skilled craftsmen in cabinet-work is continually on the wane, because of the huge salaries being offered in this computer and electronic age to high school and college graduates, by business organizations. There is little incentive to enter the craftsman's trade, because demand for his work has dwindled. What was once essential to every community is now the hobby of few and the profession of still fewer.

Much as a child resents the admonitions of his parents, the modern furniture designer rejects the authoritative precepts of the master cabinet-makers of the past. In this age of ever-widening generation gap, typified by lack of communication within the family and students rebelling against time-worn pedagogy, there is much furniture being built that is symbolic of revolt and rejection, but marred by disutility. At the same time as many criticize outmoded curriculi for not filling the needs of the present, there is much furniture being produced that, while claiming simplicity and suitability for modern needs, reveals a simple disregard for the niceties of detail.

With metals being used more and more, synthetic materials such as formica, catalin and plexiglass being featured, with liquor-proof surfaces in demand for table and bureau tops, the beauty and eloquence of wood has been lost, replaced by unrealistic materials that lack the grace and distinction of hardwoods. The modern designers defiantly proclaim their superiority: they are looking forward, not backward. But the worth of their products will be judged by the whims of public taste — what is new today may be outmoded tomorrow. One season the vogue is for Scandinavian furniture; the next, it may be Mediterranean or Spanish. Who can tell what the next years may bring?

If it seems that American furniture is being neglected, it will return with a popularity never before imagined, for we are ready to appreciate the simplicity of early taste that is at home in the modern world and has been adapted out of other styles to fit life in our climate and our country. As many young designers and homeowners are discovering, American furniture is part of our national life and can never lose favor, although some of the ornamental features appeared in response to certain periods' taste and changed to fit the times. Even the most rabid traditionalist appreciates the beauty of the unbroken line. He will admit of the magnificence that dwells in the unmolested surface. It can resemble the peace and quiet of a lake at sundown, in its satin texture.

The majesty that dwells in simplicity has never been forgotten for long. No matter how far the modernists' fancy may lead them, there still remain the fundamental laws of line, form, color, arrangement and proportions, which cannot be denied. For this reason the designer cannot really face the future without investigating the past. Basic laws governing design are just as valid today as they were when first set down by the

Greeks in their meticulous precision. Without a solid foundation the structure is wanting. Furniture design should be a natural evolution of what is worthy of the past towards the unpredictable future.

To build is more difficult than to destroy. Many modernists brutally overthrow logical development in their desire for change, repudiating centuries of study and unfolding, and abandoning 2,500 years of Western culture in their frantic search for the new. Is their only objective the destruction of the past? Or is this a product of today's adverse environment? The penury of what is being produced testifies that something is basically wrong.

There is no question that present-day developments require new and neoteric solutions. This is particularly necessary in fields that have no precedents, and there fresh deductions are inevitable. The traditionalist concurs that true progress should go on unhindered. However, one of the basic laws of physics states that to every action there is an equal and opposite reaction, and this lends understanding to what is happening today. If you walk into the showrooms of any reputable furniture establishment you will see very little of the so-called "modern" furniture displayed. Most of that is shown in the "borax" emporiums, where price is the dominant factor; but the rest of it is shown, as precious examples of plexiglass and bronze, in exclusive studios and decorator shops, at prices only the most affluent can afford.

For the people of culture and refinement, who seek out and appreciate the beauty of furniture that reflects period influences, fortunately there is no scarcity of this type of furniture; splendid reproductions may also be had, at reasonable price. There are authentic recreations being made of models from the Williamsburg restoration and from Historic Newport. Certainly there would be no justification for their obsolescence — furniture of good design and lasting beauty, when well constructed and finished for good living, will ever find a ready market.

The dictum of today seems to be speed, change and "get it done." No wonder people are uneasy, petulant and disenchanted, if they believe the past irrelevant, the present disheartening, and the future unreliable. People must accept the fact that progress is slow but the abilities and ideas of everyone working together are needed to solve the maze of problems. In the same manner, the furniture designers must acquaint themselves with the best work of the past, in order to proceed and solve the needs of the people of the present. From this perspective the heights of modern design are accessible: the prophet of what is to come is the man who understands both past and present.

INDEX

(Asterisks after page numbers refer to measured drawings)

Index of Museums, Collections and Displays